Southern Soups & Stews

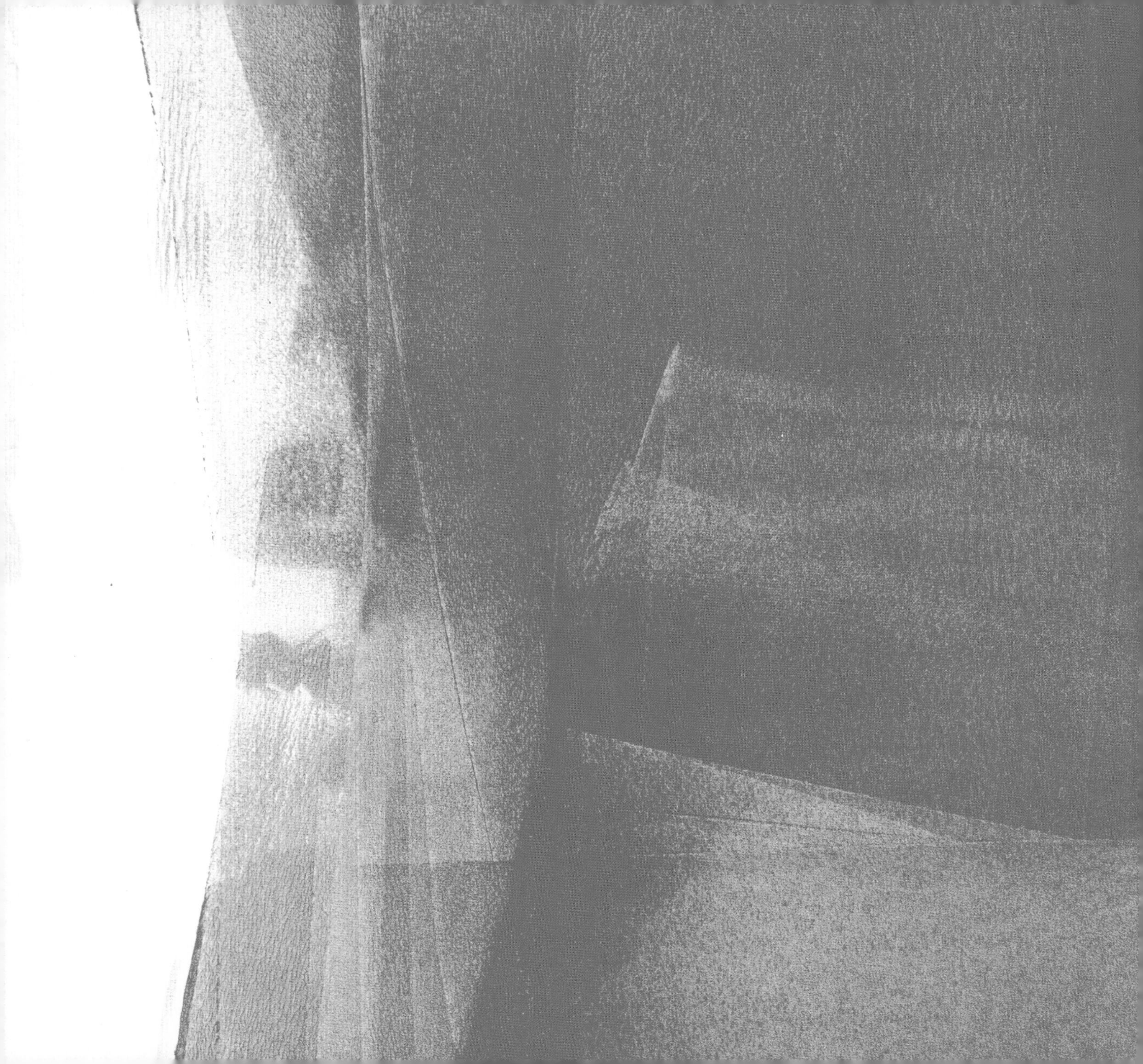

NANCIE McDERMOTT

PHOTOGRAPHS BY LEIGH BEISCH

CHRONICLE BOOKS

SAN FRANCISCO

Library of Congress Cataloging-in-Publication Data available.
ISBN 978-1-4521-2485-8

Manufactured in China

Designed by Christy Sheppard Knell
Prop styling by Sara Slavin
Food styling by Daniel Becker

10 9 8 7 6 5 4 3 2 1

Chronicle Books LLC
680 Second Street
San Francisco, California 94107
www.chroniclebooks.com

Dedication

To my friend Debbie Gooch, who introduced me to Dean and Sel, invited me to join the dorm-room cooking club, took me along on my first trip to New York City, and brought me home to Reidsville for my first Brunswick stew. Thank you for stirring the pot and seasoning it just right, then and now.

Introduction

hroughout the region we now call the American South, long before anyone put a sharpened feather to parchment paper and penned observations about it, nourishing soups and hearty stews were bubbling away on wood-fueled fires. In ceramic vessels, redware stewpots, three-legged pipkins, bulge pots, and enameled Dutch ovens, Southern cooks have been simmering and stirring for centuries, adjusting the heat of campfires, stoking the embers on open hearths, and feeding sticks into wood-burning cast-iron stoves. They were stewing and braising, winter and summer, long before the counties, towns, and states we now call home showed up on any map. Cherokee, Lumbee, Tuscarora, Seminole, and Choctaw people cooked fresh and dried beans, squash, hominy, and green corn. Newcomers from the British Isles, Europe, West Africa, and the Caribbean Islands cooked greens, field peas, potatoes, and pumpkins, stretching wild game, shellfish, and salted meats to satisfy an abundance of eaters around great tables. They paired their long-tended handiwork with corn cakes, grits, biscuits, and rice. As the nation grew, this process of invention and evolution grew right along with it, creating a culinary repertoire of soups and stews that continues to this day.

We dip our spoons into a Cajun-style gumbo; savor a layered muddle of snapper, potatoes, onions, and poached eggs; feast on okra soup colored with red-ripe tomatoes; eat hoppin' John for luck on New Year's Day. With each bite, each sip, each stir, we are tending a bed of gently glowing coals—embers from a fire lit long ago and nurtured over time by many hands. By keeping the stewpots of the historical Southern kitchen bubbling, we encourage remembrance and fuel creativity. We feed our spirits while planting seeds saved from long-ago harvests. Cooking and eating together helps us keep the old ways vibrant, and visible, where we can adapt them to suit what we have now; what we need and want—what we are hungry for today.

This book is a handbook, a workbook, and a playbook designed to help you celebrate the region's culinary traditions, the multiple and varied ways of working in the kitchens, gardens, farms, and wild spaces of the South. My goal is to feed your curiosity—to spark your interest as well as your appetite for wonderful home cooking, plain and fancy. These recipes provide you with a sampler, an initial tour of the Southern culinary landscape, lifting up various ways we feed ourselves and our dear ones with big, bold, substantial, and satisfying servings of braises and broths, dumplings and gravies, bisques and boils, soups and stews.

But how to organize it, how to come at the oversize, multifaceted subject of Southern soups and stews in a way that clarifies it, increases understanding and knowledge, and sparks interest? Regional distinctions within Southern cooking have always fascinated me, so that is the first approach I considered. On this aspect of Southern cooking, they are abundant. There are so many distinctions within a region or subregion that such a focus creates confusion. Even within one region and one community within that

What makes this gumbo "Cajun," or that dish "Creole"? These are complex unresolved questions for which there are numerous answers and ideas, in regard to the term *Creole* in particular. People just do not agree, and after pondering and exploring the issue as I wrote this book, my conclusion is this: It does not matter. Rules about what goes into a Cajun gumbo or a Creole gumbo are easy to find if you go hunting for data; but not one of them held up. Particular people insist that this ingredient would never be in such-and-such a recipe, or that ingredient would always be in that one, and then here comes a fine version that breaks that rule. To me, it doesn't matter and won't be solved here. In this book, when I say it's a Creole gumbo, it's because the person whose gumbo it is or on which it is based is Creole. Same for Cajun. And that is good enough for me.

region, variations bubble up to the top of the pot. Legendary chef Paul Prudhomme speaks fondly about growing up in the heart of Cajun country, the town of Opelousas, Louisiana, feasting on boudin, tasso, andouille sausage, and other forms of porky goodness. He looked forward to family expeditions to another heart of Cajun country, down on the bayous and along the Gulf Coast, where his equally Cajun cousins shared their corner of the country's abundance of seafood: fresh shrimp, oysters, and a variety of fish. Even within the Cajun tradition, variations appear and absolutes dissolve like sugar in hot tea. Chef Paul's own family gumbos included both superbly fresh seafood from his bayou-based Cajun family members and hearty spice-infused sausages and meat from his own family of upcountry Cajuns. Surf and turf, powerfully seasoned and shared with pleasure—all within one Cajun family.

HOW ABOUT A HISTORICAL APPROACH? There's a tempting one, given the span of four centuries during which the South has been home to bubbling pots of stew. A seasonal approach could work as well, arranging soup and stew recipes into a Southern cook's almanac. I could move from dried beans and salt pork in February to freshly picked English peas with silken dumplings in late spring; from okra soup with juicy tomatoes in August to massive pots of Brunswick stew and burgoo, cooked and stirred outdoors, come fall.

Or perhaps a cultural calendar, approaching the subject through signature soups and stews linked to celebrations and rituals. Creole cooks in New Orleans cook up gumbo z'herbes on Holy Thursday, and families in the Piedmont of North Carolina, pry open oysters aplenty for the Christmas Eve tradition of oyster stew. Then we could go back to New Orleans for the Monday tradition of red beans and rice. Up until the mid-twentieth century, Mondays were washdays, and the demanding work of doing a household's laundry by hand left cooks little time to prepare the evening meal. The solution was to put a big pot of red beans with sausage and spices on the stove as a back-burner supper. Creole red beans bubbled away all day, providing everyone with a satisfying and substantial supper at day's end.

Then I saw the patterns on which I needed to organize the story. They're a combination of an ingredient-centered approach with a recipe-centered approach. For ingredients, crab and shrimp have their own chapter, as do fish and shellfish, general vegetables, and field peas and beans. For recipes, gumbos have their own chapter, as do dumpling-blessed soups and stews, and Brunswick stews and wild game. This gave me a path to follow, which I tested out on the two ocean and coastal chapters.

Would this approach let me cast a wide enough net for the big Southern culinary story, while focusing in on particular regions, cultural traditions, and seasonal dishes? Yes! To find that story, I started on the windy shores and inlets of Maryland's Chesapeake Bay, explored the oyster beds up the Rappahannock River, and meandered down along the coastline through Tidewater Virginia. Then I visited North Carolina's Outer Banks and barrier islands, and the Lowcountry of South Carolina and Georgia. I researched the vibrant cooking and culture of the Gullah and Geechee people of the Sea Islands, and explored Florida, with its endless coastline guiding you along the Atlantic and around to the Gulf of Mexico, where seafood-centric soups and stews tempt you from Appalachicola, Florida, across Alabama, Mississippi, Louisiana, and Texas. I'd traveled far, without even beginning to consider the bubbling cauldrons of inland Southern cooking, from West Virginia and Tennessee, Kentucky and Arkansas, the Piedmont, Great Smokies, the Blue Ridge, and all the goodness of the Mountain South. But those regions had a chance to shine and take center stage when I developed the chapters on dumplings; beans and field peas; and beef, chicken, and pork stews.

Once I had my approach, I put on my detective hat and got out my magnifying glass for the research and pondering, exploring and curating that I love. This led to cooking, more questions, more cooking, reading, sifting, and sorting, until what you find here came together, not in one big pot, but in a mighty buffet of words, pictures, recipes, and understanding.

I ended up where I started—in love with this old-time, essentially simple, intrinsically generous way of cooking, of making good use of what you have. The equipment is everyday, and the techniques are

If you find yourself in a vegetable-specific spelling bee, know this: not everybody knows how to spell "butterbeans." The tiny, delicately green, plump and creamy little legumes show up in Southern gardens in late May, and disappear into pots, serving dishes, and tummies as fast as we can shell them and simmer them to tenderness with something porky and salty. Shelled and packed into pint and quart bags, they cost more than the unshelled ones, but plenty of us gladly pay for the time and skill required to split open each flat, curved pod. Some dictionaries prefer "butter beans," and some even claim that they are simply lima beans by another name. Here in the Piedmont of North Carolina, the two-word version is acceptable, but on cardboard signs at produce stands, it's "butterbeans" all the way.

commonsense, well within the skill set of anyone who wants to put a meal together and bring it to the table with contentment and pride. The flavors are varied and timeless; not trendy, not effortful, but real, true, and good. These are dishes that have lasted over time, pleased a wide array of people, and put what is before us to good and nourishing use.

This way of cooking and these recipes bring out good things in people. Southerners didn't invent soups and stews; nobody did. Yet we've always known a good thing when we saw it, and nature and luck have given us the accidental good fortune to live surrounded by culinary inspiration. Our growing season is long, from early spring to late fall, and even in winter there are those collard greens out in the field, no longer growing but pretty much able to weather the winter's storms. In many places the soil is good enough, the sun and rain and temperatures are kind enough, to make peach and apple orchards thrive, to make muscadine and scuppernong grape arbors groan, and to allow us to keep a little vegetable garden and raise a few animals on grassy pastures.

WE'VE BEEN LUCKY, AND WE LOVE TO SHARE THAT. You don't need to be Southern to enjoy these dishes. I hope you will cook them, and find some of them to your liking. May these recipes inspire you to think about the soups and stews that matter to you, recipes and dishes from your world, your family, your culture or time or place. Consider your past, or the place you call home now. Consider your traditions, and if you like them and find them worthy, share them. Teach them to someone who might enjoy them now and cherish them later. If you don't really have traditions or don't care for the ones life assigned to you, head to your kitchen and make up some new ones. Adoption has always been a lovely way to create connections, and new combinations can create strength, beauty, and surprises. Here's to cooking these Southern soups and stews in your kitchen; to eating them with people whose company you enjoy. Here's to stirring the pots and filling the bowls; to sharing what we have, what we know, and what we love.

1

Gumbos

FROM PICNIC TABLES AT A *BOUCHERIE* (butchery) in Cajun country to the damask-covered tables in a French Quarter dining room, from a kitchen table in Mobile to one in Charleston or on nearby Edisto Island, gumbos reign supreme. Rich in history and varied in type, gumbos stir up discussion and sometimes disagreements, from the definition of a gumbo to from whence it came.

Nearly everyone concurs that gumbo in any form is an extraordinary, hearty, and delicious stew, teeming with robust flavors, redolent with herbs and spices, richly deserving of its popularity, and worthy of attention and respect. As to what exactly goes in it and how it should properly be made? Let the contradictory opinions flow forth, beginning with origins and ingredients and continuing through technique and how it should be accompanied and served. The only absolute truth regarding gumbo is that nobody anywhere can absolutely and definitively explain it, define it, or claim it. This dish looms larger than any one group's understanding of it, because its roots lead in many directions: West Africa and the Caribbean; France and Acadiana; Cajun country and Creole culture in New Orleans; Mobile, Alabama, parts of Florida, and the Mississippi Delta; and down to the Gulf of Mexico. *Gumbo* means what it means in each region where people still love it and make it and care enough about it to define it for themselves. Gumbo is more complex and vibrant than any one serving of words printed on any one page.

This chapter presents you with a gumbo primer, strongly seasoned by the most familiar version in modern Southern culture, the Cajun-style, roux-based gumbos of Louisiana, lifted into the national spotlight in the 1980s by Chef Paul Prudhomme. When he opened his French Quarter restaurant, K-Paul's Louisiana Kitchen, people fell in love with the extraordinary, intensely flavored cooking, based on his Cajun roots. Chef Paul introduced the popular term "the Trinity" to describe the three modern essential seasonings for Cajun-style gumbos: onion, celery, and bell pepper, all chopped up and added to a roux once it reached its proper color, to cook their flavor into the dish and halt the browning of said roux. Chef Paul compares these seasonings to the French tradition of beginning many dishes with a mirepoix, a mixture of finely chopped onions, celery, and carrots rather than the green peppers used in Louisiana's kitchens.

We begin with such a Cajun-style gumbo, using andouille sausage and chicken. Next come three okra-based Creole-style gumbos, from legendary Creole chefs. Two of these culinary leaders, Lena Richard and Henry Carr, have passed away. One, Chef Leah Chase, is a living national treasure whose wonderful restaurant, Dooky Chase, still features her famous gumbo z'herbes on Holy Thursday each year. You'll also find two more Louisiana variations on the gumbo theme, plus two gumbos with Afro-Caribbean roots, one historical version from nineteenth-century entrepreneur and cookbook author Mrs. Abby Fisher, and the other from Nathalie Dupree, whose book *Mastering the Art of Southern Cooking* encompasses her lifetime of culinary knowledge on every aspect of Southern ingredients, techniques, and recipes. This book's intention is not to settle the questions or take sides, but rather to celebrate, illuminate, and get people into the kitchen to cook gumbos, as well as support the delicious creations served up by all those gumbo-makers out there in the wide world. On your mark, get set, gumbo!

Serves 8

Marcelle Bienvenu's Shrimp and Egg Gumbo

Beloved as the ever-flowing fountain of classic and contemporary recipes for Louisiana's extraordinary cuisine, Marcelle Bienvenu is widely regarded as the Queen of Cajun Cuisine. Born and raised in the town of St. Martinville on Bayou Teche, she was exposed to journalism and great cooking early on, with a father who established the town's first newspaper and an extended family of women who cooked creatively and brilliantly. In her many books and long-running columns for the *Times-Picayune* of New Orleans and NOLA.com, she explores history and traditions while staying open to inspiration. Intrigued by a classic Cajun gumbo recipe she learned from the late chef Eula Mae Dore, she came up with this summertime gumbo using fresh shrimp and finely chopped hard-boiled eggs. When it's too hot to work on a meaty gumbo, she puts this on to simmer and ends up with a satisfying rice-and-gumbo supper.

- ½ cup vegetable oil
- ⅔ cup all-purpose flour
- 1 cup chopped yellow onions
- ½ cup chopped celery
- ¼ cup chopped green bell pepper
- 2 quarts Shrimp Stock (page 153) or water
- 1 teaspoon salt
- ½ teaspoon cayenne pepper
- 1 pound medium shrimp, peeled and deveined
- 8 large eggs
- ½ cup chopped green onions
- ½ cup chopped fresh parsley
- Everyday Rice (page 154) for serving

1 In a large, heavy pot or a Dutch oven, heat the vegetable oil over medium heat for 2 minutes. When a pinch of flour blooms on the surface when added to the oil, scatter in the flour and stir quickly and thoroughly, combining the oil and flour evenly into a thick, smooth roux. Continue cooking, stirring often, as the roux darkens from white to ivory to a rich, medium brown, the color of peanut butter, 15 to 20 minutes.

2 Add the onions and continue stirring, cooking the roux for 1 minute more. Add the celery and bell pepper and cook, stirring constantly, for 2 minutes more.

3 Pour in 2 cups of the stock, and stir to mix it in evenly. Pour in the remaining 6 cups stock and continue stirring to combine everything. Turn the heat to medium-low, cover the pot, and let simmer gently, stirring occasionally, for 1½ hours.

4 Uncover and stir in the salt and cayenne. Use a large spoon to skim off any oil that has risen to the surface. Increase the heat to medium and let come to a boil. Add the shrimp and stir them into the gumbo. Cook until the shrimp change color, 1 to 2 minutes.

5 Break one of the eggs into a small bowl and slide it gently into the gumbo. Repeat with the remaining seven eggs, adding them carefully all around the sides of the pot. Do not stir the gumbo. Scatter the green onions and parsley over the gumbo and cover. Simmer for 10 minutes more. Serve the gumbo in deep soup bowls with rice.

Serves 6 to 8

In her adopted city of Charleston, South Carolina, beloved cookbook author and television cooking star Nathalie Dupree celebrates culinary traditions of the Lowcountry, along with those of her native Georgia and the rest of the South. Unlike the roux-based, pepper-fueled gumbos of Louisiana, her Atlantic coast gumbo features okra and tomatoes and has no dark-colored roux as a base. While bacon grease is the sole meaty ingredient in this recipe, Nathalie notes that this recipe is a template that you can revise to suit yourself. Ms. Dupree is the author of thirteen cookbooks, most recently the James Beard Award–winner *Mastering the Art of Southern Cooking*. I've simplified her recipe to make enough for a family rather than a big crowd. You could double it and add a pint of oysters and a half-pound of crabmeat shortly before serving if you'd like to enjoy its full delights.

Nathalie Dupree's Lowcountry Okra and Shrimp Gumbo

- 3 tablespoons bacon grease or vegetable oil
- 5 cups sliced fresh okra
- 1 cup chopped onion
- ¾ cup chopped celery
- ½ cup chopped green bell pepper
- 1 tablespoon chopped garlic
- 1½ cups fresh or canned chopped tomatoes
- 5 cups Shrimp Stock (page 153) or Chicken Stock (page 152)
- 1 teaspoon salt
- 1 teaspoon freshly ground pepper
- ½ teaspoon cayenne pepper
- 1½ pounds medium shrimp, peeled and deveined
- ½ cup chopped green onions
- Everyday Rice (page 154) for serving

1 Heat the bacon grease over medium-high heat in a large Dutch oven or heavy-bottomed pot. Add 3 cups of the sliced okra and toss it well. Cook, stirring often to prevent it from burning, until the okra is dry and lightly browned, 5 to 10 minutes.

2 Add the onion, celery, bell pepper, and garlic and toss them well. Cook, stirring often, until the vegetables are fragrant, shiny, and softened, about 3 minutes.

3 Stir in the tomatoes and stock. Add the salt, pepper, and cayenne; stir and let the gumbo come to a lively boil. Lower the heat to maintain a gentle simmer and cook, stirring occasionally, for 30 minutes.

4 Increase the heat to medium-high and bring the gumbo back to a gentle boil. Add the remaining 2 cups okra and cook it for 5 minutes more. Add the shrimp and cook just until the shrimp turn pink and are cooked through, about 1 minute. Stir in the green onions. Remove from the heat and serve the gumbo hot or warm with rice.

Serves 8 to 10

Henry Carr's Creole Gumbo

This classic Creole gumbo comes from *Creole Feast: 15 Master Chefs of New Orleans Reveal Their Secrets*, written by Dr. Rudolph Lombard and Chef Nathaniel Burton in 1978. A tribute to the knowledge and dedication of more than a dozen masterful guardians of the city's cuisine, the book shares anecdotes and advice from culinary geniuses, men and women who shared their secrets with generosity and pride. Chef Henry D. Carr Sr. manned the stoves at The Ponchartrain, The Court of Two Sisters, Brennan's, and Pascal's Manale during his thirty-year career, and spoke about the importance of timing, attention to detail, and flavorful stock in creating excellent gumbo the Creole way. Chef Carr sought to develop layers of flavor by including dried shrimp and gumbo crabs in his stock, and advised sautéing the okra in butter to enhance its texture and taste. His gumbos included tomatoes and an array of seafood, with a flourish of shrimp and lump crabmeat stirred in just before serving time.

¼ cup butter
¾ pound okra, caps and tips trimmed and cut into ½-inch pieces
¾ cup vegetable oil
¾ cup all-purpose flour
1½ cups chopped onion
¾ cup chopped celery
¾ cup chopped green bell pepper
¾ cup chopped green onions
1¼ cups chopped canned tomatoes or peeled fresh tomatoes, with juice
9 cups simmering Shrimp Stock (page 153), Chicken Stock (page 152), or water
Dash of Tabasco sauce or other hot pepper sauce
Dash of Worcestershire sauce
1 teaspoon salt
1 teaspoon freshly ground pepper
2 pounds medium shrimp, shelled and deveined
1 pound cooked lump crabmeat, picked over for shells
Everyday Rice (page 154) for serving
3 tablespoons filé powder (optional)

1 In a large, heavy-bottomed skillet, melt the butter over medium-high heat. When it is very bubbly and just about to brown, scatter in the okra and spread it out in a single layer. Cook it, undisturbed, until the okra is lightly browned on the bottom, and then toss it well. Continue cooking, tossing occasionally, until all the okra is lightly browned and somewhat dry, 3 to 5 minutes. Remove it from the heat and set aside.

2 In a large, heavy-bottomed Dutch oven, heat the vegetable oil over medium-high heat until shimmering hot. When a pinch of flour blooms on the surface when added to the oil, scatter in the flour and stir quickly and thoroughly, combining the oil and flour evenly into a thick, smooth roux. Continue cooking, stirring often, as the roux turns from white to ivory to a rich, medium brown, the color of peanut butter, 15 to 20 minutes.

3 Add the onion, celery, bell pepper, and about one-third of the green onions to the Dutch oven and stir quickly, mixing the vegetables into the roux. Cook, stirring often, until the vegetables are fragrant and softened, 2 to 3 minutes. Add the tomatoes and their juice and cook, stirring to mix everything together, 1 minute more.

4 Carefully pour the hot stock into the roux mixture and stir well. Add the cooked okra, Tabasco, Worcestershire, salt, and pepper. Stir well, bring the gumbo to a gentle boil, and then adjust the heat to maintain the gentle boil. Cook, stirring occasionally, for 45 minutes.

5 Add the shrimp and cook it for 5 minutes, stirring now and then. Add the crabmeat and remaining green onions, and cook for 3 minutes more, stirring gently to mix them into the gumbo. Remove from the heat and serve the gumbo hot or warm, with rice, passing the filé powder at the table to add as desired.

Serves 8 to 10

Lena Richard's Gumbo Filé

Remember this name: Lena Richard. She's the most impressive businessperson, celebrity chef, educator, television personality, and entrepreneur we never heard of. She belongs in the Hall of Fame and Glory for too many reasons to count, but for now we have mostly her recipes from which to learn about her life and work. Born in New Roads, Louisiana, in 1892, this African American woman cooked up a spectacularly successful career in the first half of the twentieth century, starring in her own twice-weekly cooking show, self-publishing a 350-recipe cookbook so impressive that a national publisher picked it up; founding a cooking school, a catering business, and a frozen-food production company; and starting and running four restaurants in New Orleans. All this in fifty-eight years. Ms. Richard passed away in 1950. Her published work, *The New Orleans Cookbook*, remains in print and makes a fine place to start considering her life and work. I love her recipe for gumbo filé, a Creole gumbo calling for "lake shrimp and crab in a golden-brown roux." I've used crabmeat instead of gumbo crabs, and added parsley and green onions. As Ms. Richard suggested, I serve this with rice.

- 5 tablespoons vegetable oil
- ½ pound boneless pork, such as Boston butt, shoulder, or pork chops, sliced into ½-inch strips
- 1 pound medium shrimp, shelled and deveined
- 3 tablespoons all-purpose flour
- 1 cup chopped onion
- 2 quarts Chicken Stock (page 152)
- 2 cups chopped, cooked chicken
- 1 teaspoon chopped garlic
- 1 bay leaf
- ½ pound cooked lump crabmeat, picked over for shells
- ¼ cup chopped green onions
- 2 tablespoons finely chopped fresh parsley
- 1 teaspoon salt
- ½ teaspoon freshly ground pepper
- Everyday Rice (page 154) for serving
- 1 tablespoon filé powder (optional)

1 In a large Dutch oven, heat 4 tablespoons of the vegetable oil over medium-high heat. Scatter in the pork and cook it undisturbed until browned, 1 to 2 minutes. Turn to cook the other side until nicely browned. Toss well and use a slotted spoon to scoop the pork into a medium bowl, leaving as much oil behind as possible.

2 Add the shrimp and cook, tossing twice, just until most of the shrimp have turned a bright pink. Scoop them out and add them to the pork. Add the remaining 1 tablespoon oil and swirl the pot to heat it.

3 When a pinch of flour blooms on the surface when added to the oil, scatter in the flour and stir quickly and thoroughly, combining the oil and flour evenly into a thick, smooth roux. Continue cooking, stirring often, until the roux releases a nutty fragrance and turns a light brown, 5 to 10 minutes.

4 Add the onion and cook, tossing often, until it releases its fragrance, softens, and is evenly coated with the roux, about 2 minutes.

5 Add the chicken stock to the pot and stir well. Add the partially cooked pork and shrimp, along with the chicken, garlic, bay leaf, and half the crabmeat. Stir and bring them to a gentle boil. Lower the heat to maintain a gentle but active simmer and cook, stirring now and then, for 20 minutes.

6 Stir in the remaining crabmeat, the green onions, parsley, salt, and pepper. Cook, stirring once or twice, until the crabmeat is heated through, about 1 minute more. Remove from the heat and serve the gumbo hot or warm, with rice, passing the filé powder at the table to add as desired.

Serves 10 to 12

Turkey Bone Gumbo

Turkey bone gumbo is Louisiana's way of extending the gratitude that flows forth on Thanksgiving Day. Smoked, deep-fried, or oven-roasted, a turkey carcass or two is the perfect reason or excuse to make a Louisiana-style gumbo, and extend gratefulness through the weekend. Thrifty and a wise use of resources, turkey bone gumbo starts with a marvelous stock produced by simmering meaty turkey bones in water for a few hours, beginning on the Friday morning after Thanksgiving. If you love big bold flavors and letting the good times roll, leave some meat on the carcass, and let this satisfying stew be the follow-up to your Thursday feast. Enjoy this seasonal gumbo with rice or potato salad. You might also enjoy warming up some leftover dressing and passing the French bread.

TURKEY STOCK

- 1 turkey carcass, preferably a meaty one, skin and all (see Note)
- 1 large or 3 small onions, unpeeled, quartered
- 3 celery stalks, cut into 3-inch chunks
- 3 carrots, cut into 3-inch chunks
- 3 bay leaves
- 1 teaspoon salt
- 1 teaspoon freshly ground pepper

- ¾ cup vegetable oil
- ¾ cup all-purpose flour
- 1 cup chopped onion
- ½ cup chopped celery
- ½ cup chopped green bell pepper
- 1 tablespoon chopped garlic
- 2 cups bite-size chunks andouille sausage or smoked kielbasa
- 1 teaspoon salt
- 1 teaspoon cayenne pepper
- ½ teaspoon freshly ground pepper
- 3 to 4 cups coarsely chopped cooked turkey, light and dark meat
- ¼ cup chopped green onions
- ¼ cup chopped fresh parsley
- Everyday Rice (page 154) for serving

1 To make the turkey stock: Place the turkey carcass in a large stockpot. Add the onion to the pot along with the celery, carrots, bay leaves, salt, and pepper.

2 Add enough water to cover the carcass by 1 to 2 inches. Break the carcass apart if necessary to fit it into the pot. Bring to a rolling boil over medium-high heat. Lower the heat to maintain a lively simmer and cook, uncovered, for 1 to 2 hours. No need to stir.

3 Remove the pot from the heat and let it cool to room temperature. Pour the stock through a fine-mesh strainer or a colander into a large bowl or another large pot. Discard all the bones and seasonings and the thick, cloudy liquid at the very bottom of the pot. Cover and refrigerate the stock. You will have 8 to 10 cups of turkey stock.

4 In a large heavy-bottomed pot or skillet, warm the vegetable oil over medium-high heat until shimmering hot. When a pinch of flour blooms on the surface when added to the oil, scatter in the flour and stir quickly and thoroughly, combining the oil and flour evenly into a thick, smooth roux. Continue cooking, stirring often, as the roux turns from off-white to beige to a rich, medium brown, the color of peanut butter, 25 to 35 minutes.

5 Add the chopped onion and keep stirring, mixing it in and letting it slow the roux down as it begins to soften, 2 to 3 minutes. Add the celery and bell pepper and stir, cooking them for about 3 minutes more, until all the seasonings have released their fragrance and are wilting nicely into the roux.

6 Add the garlic and sausage and cook, stirring often, until they also release their fragrance and start flavoring the roux, about 2 minutes.

7 Add 3 cups of the turkey stock and stir gently to help the roux and seasonings dissolve into the stock. When the roux bubbles to a gentle, steady boil, carefully add another 5 cups stock, along with the salt, cayenne, and pepper. Stir to combine everything and then let the gumbo come to a lively boil. Adjust the heat to maintain an active but gentle simmer and cook, stirring now and then, for 1 hour.

8 Add the turkey meat, stir well, and cook for 10 minutes more. Stir in the green onions and parsley. Remove from the heat, and serve the gumbo hot or warm, with plenty of rice.

NOTE: *If you begin with a smoked turkey, consider leaving out the skin, as its smoky goodness tends to take over. Instead, you could use it to make a small pot of smoked-turkey stock, to be frozen and pulled out as the inspiration for a post-holiday-season soup or stew.*

Serves 10 to 12

Chicken and Sausage Gumbo, Cajun-Style

Chocolate brown, earthy, and spiked with thyme and three kinds of pepper, this gumbo earns back every second of effort you put into the pot, from chopping your seasonings and measuring out spices to stirring away on your roux. If you make it and serve it straightaway, you will be glad you didn't have to wait to savor it. If you can cook it a day in advance, you will love how its flavors blossom. A bit of a resting time in the refrigerator allows your gumbo to cut loose, to stretch out, to meander from tasty to operatically magnificent. It means that as serving time approaches, you have had the opportunity to rest up, cook some rice, set out some libations, and crank up some music. You and your guests will surely want to dance; it is just that good. While rice is the classic gumbo accompaniment, you may enjoy the highly favored Louisiana alternative of sweet and creamy Creole potato salad with your gumbo: It's another extraordinary way to go.

- 1 cup vegetable oil
- 1 cup all-purpose flour
- 1 cup chopped onion
- 1 cup finely chopped celery
- 1 cup finely chopped green bell pepper
- 2 tablespoons finely chopped garlic
- 2 teaspoons dried thyme, or 2 tablespoons finely chopped fresh thyme
- 1 teaspoon salt
- 1 teaspoon freshly ground pepper
- 1 teaspoon sweet or hot paprika
- 1 teaspoon cayenne pepper
- 2 quarts Chicken Stock (page 152)
- 3½ pounds skin-on, bone-in chicken legs and thighs
- 1 pound Cajun-style andouille sausage, smoked kielbasa, or other smoked sausage
- 1 cup thinly sliced green onions, plus more for garnish
- ½ cup finely chopped fresh parsley
- Everyday Rice (page 154) for serving

1 In a large, heavy-bottomed Dutch oven, preferably cast iron or enamel cast iron, or a large cast-iron skillet, heat the vegetable oil over medium-high heat until shimmering hot. When a pinch of flour blooms on the surface when added to the oil, scatter in the flour and stir quickly and thoroughly, combining the oil and flour evenly into a thick, smooth roux. Continue cooking, stirring often, as the roux turns from pale yellow to a rich, deep brown, 20 to 35 minutes. Adjust the heat as needed to keep the roux darkening slowly, without bubbling up or burning. It should be darker than peanut butter, about the color of coffee with some cream, a deep brown but not a dark brown.

2 Add the onion, celery, and bell pepper to the Dutch oven and stir well, heating them up and coating them with the roux. Let them cook, stirring often, until the vegetables are fragrant, softened, shiny, and evenly coated with the roux, 2 to 3 minutes. Add the garlic, thyme, salt, pepper, paprika, and cayenne; stir well and cook for 2 minutes more. If using a cast-iron skillet, transfer the roux to a large stockpot. →

3 Add the chicken stock, stir well, and bring it to a lively boil, stirring often to dissolve the roux into the stock. When everything is boiling nicely, add the chicken pieces. When the stock returns to a rolling boil, adjust the heat to maintain a lively simmer and cook, stirring now and then, until the chicken is cooked through and very tender, 45 minutes to 1 hour.

4 Meanwhile, chop the andouille into bite-size pieces. Halve each link lengthwise, and then cut it crosswise into half-moon slices about ¼ inch thick.

5 Remove the chicken from the pot and set it out on a platter to cool. As soon as it is cool enough to touch, pull the meat from the bones, discarding the bones and skin. Tear or chop the chicken very coarsely, and then return the meat to the pot. Add the andouille and stir. Cook, stirring now and then, until the sausage has seasoned the gumbo and softened, and everything has come together into a rich, flavorful, slightly thickened stew, about 30 minutes more.

6 Remove the pot from the heat and stir in the green onions and parsley. Serve the gumbo in bowls over rice or with rice on the side, garnished with green onions.

Serves 8 to 10

Bring on the greens! This unique, classic gumbo showcases those nutritious, robust, and flavorful leafy vegetables we need to consume often and in abundance. Collards, cabbage, watercress, and the tops of carrots, turnips, and beets shine in this meat-and-vegetables concoction. It's traditionally served on Holy Thursday before the Good Friday fast, which Roman Catholic teaching requires. Chef Leah Chase cooks huge quantities of this gumbo annually, and New Orleanians flock to Dooky Chase restaurant for her signature dish. When Hurricane Katrina flooded her landmark restaurant in 2005, she vowed to reopen, ideally by Holy Thursday the following year. With repairs incomplete, the indomitable chef did the next best thing, cooking and serving her first post-Katrina gumbo z'herbes in the parking lot in 2006. Chef Chase urges an easygoing attitude toward this recipe. Greens can include Swiss chard, dandelion greens, creasie greens, romaine, or arugula instead of those she's listed, and while using an odd number of greens is considered good luck, she urges us to keep a light heart and do the best we can, even or odd. This is my small-scale version of Ms. Chase's mighty fine stew.

Leah Chase's Gumbo z'Herbes

GREENS

6 cups coarsely chopped collard greens

5 cups coarsely chopped mustard greens

4 cups coarsely chopped turnip greens

3 cups coarsely chopped watercress

3 cups coarsely chopped spinach

3 cups coarsely chopped lettuce

2 cups coarsely chopped cabbage

2 cups coarsely chopped beet tops

1 cup coarsely chopped carrot tops

2 cups coarsely chopped onions

⅓ cup chopped garlic

MEATS

½ pound smoked sausage, such as andouille, chopped into 1-inch chunks

½ pound smoked ham, chopped into 1-inch chunks

½ pound beef brisket, chopped into 1-inch chunks

½ pound beef stew meat, chopped into 1-inch chunks

⅓ cup vegetable oil

½ pound hot spicy sausage, such as chaurice or chorizo, chopped into bite-size pieces

3 tablespoons all-purpose flour

1 teaspoon dried thyme, or 1 tablespoon fresh thyme leaves

1 teaspoon salt

½ teaspoon cayenne pepper

Everyday Rice (page 154) for serving

Filé powder (optional)

1 To make the greens: Combine all the greens in a 12-quart stockpot. Add the onions, garlic, and enough water to cover the greens by 1 inch. Place the stockpot over medium-high heat and bring it to a rolling boil, then adjust the heat to maintain a lively but gentle boil and cook for 30 minutes. The greens will cook down and become tender. Use tongs or a long-handled spoon to stir the greens now and then as they simmer.

2 When the greens are very tender, remove the pot from the heat. Let it stand until the pot cools down enough to handle, 30 minutes or so. Meanwhile, place a large strainer or a colander over another large cooking pot or bowl. Strain the greens cooking liquid into the other pot, and set the cooked greens aside on a platter or in a large bowl to cool to room temperature. →

3 To make the meats: Put the smoked sausage, ham, beef brisket, and beef stew meat in the stock-pot and add about 1 quart of the cooking liquid from the greens, reserving the remaining liquid. Place the pot over medium-high heat and bring it to a lively boil. Lower the heat to maintain an active, visible simmer. Cook, stirring now and then, until all the meats are fragrant and tender, 30 to 45 minutes.

4 Meanwhile, heat the vegetable oil in a large heavy skillet over medium-high heat until hot. Scatter in the spicy sausage and cook, tossing often, until it is nicely browned and cooked through, 10 to 12 minutes. Transfer the cooked sausage to a bowl, leaving 3 tablespoons of the fat in the skillet for making the roux. (Add vegetable oil if you don't have enough.)

5 When the cooked greens are cool enough to handle, puree them in a food processor or a blender until smooth. Work in batches, taking your time and adding some of the reserved greens cooking liquid to the food processor to help grind up the greens as needed. (You could also gently squeeze the greens to release some of their cooking liquid and finely chop them by hand.)

6 Heat the grease in the skillet over medium-high heat until hot but not smoking. When a pinch of flour blooms on the surface when added to the grease, scatter in the flour and stir quickly and thoroughly, combining the grease and flour evenly into a thick, smooth roux. Continue cooking, stirring often, as the roux turns from white to lightly browned, about 5 minutes.

7 Add the roux to the pot of chopped meats and stir to mix everything well. Add the pureed greens to the pot, along with 1 quart of the greens cooking liquid. Stir to mix everything together. Place the pot over medium-high heat and bring it to a gentle boil. Adjust the heat to maintain a lively simmer and cook, stirring often, until the gumbo is pleasantly thick, fragrant, and well combined, about 20 minutes.

8 Add the reserved sausage to the gumbo along with the thyme, salt, and cayenne. Stir to mix everything together. Cook at a gentle simmer for 40 minutes more. Remove from the heat and serve the gumbo hot or warm, with rice, passing the filé powder at the table to add as desired.

Perusing the pages of *What Mrs. Fisher Knows about Old Southern Cooking*, I feel certain that I am gazing through a window into the kitchens of the early American South, between 1800 and 1860. Published in 1881, this cookbook contains the recipes, wisdom, and culinary expertise of a famous and respected entrepreneur, caterer, chef, and businessperson in San Francisco. A renowned purveyor of pickles and preserves, Mrs. Fisher obliged requests from her friends, fans, and customers for a book of her recipes, publishing this volume of information on an array of dishes from her repertoire of Southern cuisine. One of the earliest known cookbooks by an African American author, this book includes her recipe for "ochra gumbo." This is my version of her stew of beef shanks, okra, and rice. I've added a little parsley here, and I often stir in a cupful each of corn and chopped tomatoes, ingredients Mrs. Fisher used in some of her other beef soups. While we don't know where she was born and raised, we do know that Mrs. Fisher lived in Mobile, Alabama, before moving west, and that her expertise on traditional Southern cooking was appreciated and highly valued in the cosmopolitan city of San Francisco toward the end of the nineteenth century.

Serves 4 to 6

Abby Fisher's Ochra Gumbo with Beef and Rice

2½ to 3 pounds meaty beef shanks
1 teaspoon salt
1 teaspoon freshly ground pepper
4 cups sliced fresh or chopped frozen okra
3 cups Everyday Rice (page 154)
¼ cup finely chopped fresh parsley

1 In a Dutch oven or large pot, combine the beef shanks and about 10 cups water—enough to cover the shanks well. Bring them to a lively boil over medium-high heat. Skim off and discard any foam that rises to the top. After 10 minutes, lower the heat to maintain a visible simmer. Add the salt and pepper and cook, uncovered, until the meat is very tender and easy to pull apart, 1 to 2 hours.

2 Transfer the shanks to a plate and add the okra to the pot. While the okra cooks, remove the meat from the bones, chop it into bite-size pieces, and return it to the soup, along with any marrow you can scoop from the bones. Cook until the okra is tender, about 20 minutes. Stir in the rice and parsley and cook them for 1 minute more. Serve hot or warm.

2
Brunswick Stews, Kentucky Burgoo, *and* Hunter's Stews

THE GREAT STATES OF GEORGIA AND VIRGINIA have two major things in common: Each is home to its own Brunswick County, and each claims to be the home-place of the first-ever bubbling pot of that famous Southern specialty, Brunswick stew. This beloved dish begins with an array of meats—typically chicken and beef, with squirrel and rabbit often included—cooked to make a foundational broth. Supplementing the broth are tomatoes, potatoes, lima beans, corn, and a little butter at the end, with a whisper of chile peppers and a standard accompaniment of saltine crackers crumbled in or on the side.

Virginia staked her claim boldly in 1988, with a statewide proclamation as this stew's place of origin, and it has hosted an annual Brunswick stew festival and contest for more than twenty-five years. In a gesture of goodwill, they invite rival stew-masters to bring their crews up from Georgia for some spirited stew celebrations. Georgia staked her own claim by building a monument featuring a massive cast-iron stewpot, which they proudly declare to be the very one in which noble Georgia residents stirred up the very first batch of Brunswick stew back in 1898.

North Carolina has its own long-standing Brunswick stew tradition, based in the Piedmont region at the center of the state. That state's own Brunswick County pays no attention to the hubbub, and all people seem to care about is making sure they sign up to get a few quarts of stew before the supply runs out. In and around the town of Reidsville, in Rockingham

County, North Carolina, stews happen throughout the fall and winter, with church groups selling out every container and bowl, usually well in advance. Numerous worthy causes appreciate the effort involved, which allows for the funding of a food bank program, building of a playground, covering of scholarships, or the purchasing of a new fire truck for the volunteer fire department.

Over on the far side of the great Southern Appalachian mountain range, cooks in Kentucky have a longtime and strong tradition of making a very similar concoction, known as burgoo. The many similarities include the use of tomatoes, corn, and onions along with the inclusion of multiple meats; the need for many helpers for preparation, cooking, distribution, and cleanup; and the ease of getting the entire community to support a worthy cause in exchange for portions of a long-simmered, patiently stirred, classic hearty stew. One unique property of burgoo is the inclusion of mutton, both in the stew and as a double-feature, in which barbecued mutton is served up alongside the stew to huge, happy crowds. Burgoo cooks make the same stipulation about how to tell that the burgoo is done: The big wooden "paddle," used to stir for hours and keep the burgoo from sticking and burning, must stand up all by itself in the middle of the pot, proving that the stew has thickened sufficiently.

In addition to these two marquee traditions, Southern cooks have made a variety of other stews, once centered on small game hunted or captured for the family table, and more recently using beef shanks, meaty beef bones, or the occasional hambone as an inexpensive anchoring ingredient. These are more modest in the number of ingredients as well as their quantity, making family-size, indoor versions too ordinary to merit a mention in most cookbooks over the years. Particular recipes have become popular over time as a way to enjoy wild game. This chapter includes two hunter's stews—one for quail and the other for duck. If you have connections to hunters with extra game in their freezers, offer to share these dishes in exchange for some of their treasure. You can also use farm-raised quail and duck in these recipes, with incredibly tasty and pleasing results.

Serves 6 to 8

Rufus Estes' Brunswick Stew

First published in 1911, *Rufus Estes' Good Things to Eat: The First Cookbook by an African-American Chef* numbers among the earliest known volumes on food and hospitality by an African American author. Born in Murray County, Tennessee, in 1857, Mr. Estes worked in restaurants in Nashville and Chicago, becoming a porter for the Pullman Palace Car Company and then executive chef for U.S. Steel. His cookbook contains more than two hundred recipes, including roast suckling pig, duck with orange sauce, oysters *à la poulette*, Guernsey cheese soufflé, glacé figs, and raspberry shrub. Mr. Estes begins with an array of soups, including his version of Brunswick stew. What a delight to see that this Chicago-based chef, cooking for a sophisticated national and international clientele, included this rustic Southern classic along with Creole chicken gumbo, lobster bisque, lamb curry, and chestnut soup with croutons. Like most versions of Brunswick stew, his centers on chicken and calls for fresh tomatoes, butter beans, and corn cut from the cob, though he specifies that canned vegetables may be used instead. Strips of pastry added as dumplings show the home-style roots of his stew, and make for a satisfying, comforting dish.

- 1 chicken (about 4 pounds), cut into serving pieces
- 1½ teaspoons salt
- 1 teaspoon freshly ground pepper
- 3 cups peeled, coarsely chopped tomatoes
- 3 cups white or yellow corn, fresh, frozen, or canned
- 2 cups butterbeans or lima beans, fresh, frozen, or canned
- 1 cup chopped onion
- 1 cup all-purpose flour

1 Place the chicken pieces in a large Dutch oven or a stockpot and add enough water to cover. Bring it to a rolling boil over medium-high heat. Skim off and discard any foam that rises to the surface. After 10 minutes, lower the heat to maintain an active but gentle simmer. Add the salt and pepper and cook the chicken for 35 minutes.

2 Add the tomatoes, corn, butterbeans, and onion. Stir to mix everything evenly into the soup. Cook it for 25 minutes more, until the chicken is tender. Transfer the chicken pieces to a platter to cool, leaving the vegetables simmering in the stew.

3 Meanwhile, in a medium bowl, combine the flour with ⅓ cup broth from the stockpot and stir them together. You will have a raggedy bowlful of dough. Using your hands, press and scoop it into a lump and then knead it a few dozen times, until you have a fairly smooth, springy dough.

4 Using a rolling pin on a lightly floured surface, roll the dough out into a big, thin round a little thinner than pie crust. Cut it into long, slender strips, about 1 inch wide and 2 inches long, and transfer the dough to a large plate or platter by the stove.

5 Remove and discard the skin and bones from the cooled chicken pieces, and pull or chop the meat into big bite-size pieces. Return the chicken meat to the stew and stir it in. Cook it for 5 minutes more.

6 Increase the heat to high and bring the stew to a rolling boil. Drop in the dough pieces one by one, adding them around the pot without touching each other. Scoop a little broth up over the dumplings to moisten them. After 2 minutes, stir gently to move the dumplings down into the stew. When the dumplings are tender and chewy like good pasta, remove the pot from the heat. Serve the stew hot or warm.

Serves 12 to 15

My friend Wendell David Brock is a magnificently talented cook as well as a fine journalist, so when he invited me over for his mother's signature Brunswick stew, I replied with a swift and eager "Yes!" I loved every bite, even though it is not the Piedmont, North Carolina–style stew on which I was raised. Mrs. Brock's recipe reflects her roots in the state of Georgia, with the inclusion of pork and ground beef, English peas, and creamed corn. Hers is a stove-top version, though it's hardly petite. Wendell pestered his mom for her recipe just a few years back and reported, "I got worried that I would never be able to re-create the flavor of my mom's wonderful Brunswick stew. Turns out that her secret ingredient comes out of a bottle—it's Kraft Hickory Smoke Barbecue Sauce. You can use any kind of sauce you like, but your stew won't taste like Virginia Brock's." The recipe makes a considerable amount, calling for a 12-quart stockpot. I divided it into a half-portion and found myself with a perfect and still generous amount of stew, but know that you can double this if your guest or gift list requires a truly gracious plenty.

Virginia Brock's Georgia-Style Brunswick Stew

- 3½ pounds boneless pork, preferably Boston butt, shoulder, or country-style ribs
- 2 tablespoons vegetable oil
- 2 pounds ground beef
- 1 pound ground turkey
- One 28-ounce can whole peeled plum tomatoes, with juice
- One 28-ounce can chopped tomatoes, with juice
- One 20-ounce bottle hickory-smoked barbecue sauce
- One 14½-ounce can cream-style corn
- One 14½-ounce can whole-kernel corn, or 1½ cups frozen corn
- 1 tablespoon Worcestershire sauce
- 1 tablespoon hot sauce, such as Tabasco or Texas Pete
- 1 tablespoon freshly ground pepper
- 2 teaspoons salt
- Two 15-ounce cans English peas, drained, such as Le Sueur, or 2 cups frozen peas

1 Place the pork in a large stockpot or Dutch oven (cut into chunks if need be). Cover the pork with water and bring it to a boil over high heat. Skim off any foam as it rises to the top during the first 15 or 20 minutes. Then lower the heat to maintain a gentle simmer and cook until the meat is tender enough to pull apart using two forks, 2 to 3 hours.

2 When the meat is done, transfer it to a large platter and allow it to cool to room temperature. Pull it apart and chop it roughly into small pieces.

3 While the pork is cooking, heat a large skillet over medium-high heat and add the vegetable oil, swirling to coat the pan. Crumble in the ground beef and turkey and cook them, turning and pressing to cook them evenly. When all the meat is cooked through, remove it from the heat and set aside.

4 In a large Dutch oven or a stockpot, combine the pork, beef, and turkey. Add the whole and chopped tomatoes, barbecue sauce, cream-style and whole-kernel corn, Worcestershire, hot sauce, pepper, and salt. Place the pot over medium heat and bring it to a lively boil, stirring often.

5 When the stew is bubbling hot, lower the heat to maintain a gentle simmer and cook, stirring occasionally, for 1 hour and 15 minutes. Stir and scrape the bottom to prevent the stew from sticking or burning. About 5 minutes before serving time, add the peas to the stew and stir gently to mix them in evenly. Cook the stew for 5 minutes more and serve it hot.

Serves 8 to 10

Amber Nimocks's Wild Game Brunswick Stew

As a journalist, Amber Nimocks has covered crime, business, agriculture, politics, and the legal profession, but she loves turning her newsroom expertise to stories about food. Judging a Brunswick stew–cooking contest got her thinking about the role of wild game in this classic Southern dish, and *Edible Piedmont* magazine assigned her to get the story on locally sourced, wild-caught ingredients for what is known in our part of the country by one unmodified word: Stew. Since wild game can't be sold in our state, she turned to friends who are hunters, and obtained venison, rabbit, and squirrel. She made them into a traditional stew filled with tomatoes, corn, and butterbeans and served it over rice. Here's what she learned: First, she found that squirrel does not taste like chicken; the meat is darker and smoother in texture. Second, the modern-day cultural stigma around eating squirrel affected some of her guests, and prevented them from enjoying small game. Third, wild-game Brunswick stew goes very well with a good pinot noir.

- 1 squirrel, dressed (about 1 pound)
- 4 bacon slices
- 1 rabbit, dressed (about 2 pounds), cut into quarters
- Salt
- Freshly ground pepper
- 1 pound venison, preferably backstrap or tenderloin, cut into 2-inch chunks
- 4 cups fresh or frozen butterbeans or lima beans
- One 28-ounce can crushed tomatoes
- ½ cup smoky-flavored barbecue sauce
- ¼ cup Worcestershire sauce
- 1 tablespoon prepared yellow mustard
- 4½ cups fresh or frozen corn

1 Rinse the squirrel meat thoroughly. Put it in a small pot and cover it with water. Bring the water to a boil and then lower the heat to maintain a simmer for about 30 minutes.

2 Meanwhile, in a heavy-bottomed stockpot, fry the bacon until it is fragrant, browned, and crisp. Remove the cooked bacon and set it aside to add to the stew later. Leave the bacon grease in the pot.

3 Season the rabbit well with salt and pepper. Heat the bacon grease until sizzling hot, and place the rabbit pieces in the pot. Cook, turning as needed, until the rabbit is handsomely browned. Remove the pot from the heat and transfer the rabbit to a plate by the stove, leaving the drippings in the pot.

4 Season the venison well with salt and pepper. Reheat the bacon grease and brown the chunks of venison on all sides. Return the browned rabbit to the pot with the venison and set the pot aside.

5 When the squirrel is tender and cooked through, remove it from the pot to cool, reserving the stock. When cool enough to handle, pick the meat from the bones. Add it to the stockpot with the venison and rabbit, discarding the bones.

6 Add the squirrel stock to the pot, along with enough water to cover the meat. Bring the pot to a rolling boil over high heat, then lower the heat to maintain a lively simmer and cook until all the meat is tender and the stock is flavorful, about 1 hour.

7 Remove the rabbit and venison pieces from the pot, placing them on a large platter to cool to room temperature. While they cool, add the butterbeans, crushed tomatoes, barbecue sauce, Worcestershire, and mustard to the pot and stir well. Let the stew simmer while you prepare the cooked meats.

8 When the rabbit is cool enough to handle, remove and discard the bones, and add the rabbit meat back to the stockpot with the squirrel. Chop the venison into smaller pieces and add it to the stew as well. Crumble in the reserved bacon.

9 Add the corn and stir. Cook until all the ingredients are tender and evenly seasoned, and the stew has thickened a little, about 20 minutes more. Serve it hot or warm.

Makes about 15 gallons of stew; about 150 servings

Benton Gooch's Outdoor Old-School Brunswick Stew

Back in the day, when my friend Debbie Gooch and I were students at the University of North Carolina at Chapel Hill, she invited me to her home one October weekend for the familiar autumn endeavor known as "having a stew." A traditional cooking event undertaken by families and institutions throughout the Piedmont, North Carolina from up into Virginia and down into South Carolina and Georgia, "having a stew" denotes a marathon cooking session requiring many hands, many hours, many chickens, and an abundance of summer vegetables picked and preserved specifically for the stewpot come fall. From this bounty, families, church groups, civic clubs, and volunteer fire departments cook up and dish out a winter's worth of one-dish suppers using nothing but widely available ingredients, elbow grease, and time. Recipes abound, and while arguments might flare up over whether the name "Brunswick" denotes origins in so-named towns and counties in Virginia, North Carolina, or Georgia, nobody really cares about that and everybody knows exactly what it is: a simple, hearty stew made with multiple meats, originally including squirrel and rabbit, but now centered on stewing chickens and beef. It requires tomatoes, onions, lima beans, and corn; and it needs serious, constant stirring so that it doesn't stick to the cauldron and burn while cooking for a very long time. I clearly remember phase one of the tradition: sitting around the kitchen table on that Friday afternoon, helping Debbie, her sister, and her mother pick a dozen or so cooked chickens. That meant pulling the meat off the bones and setting it aside, while discarding bones and skin. This picked chicken and other ingredients went into Mr. Gooch's 25-gallon cast-iron wash pot in the backyard to cook over a wood fire all night long. I slept through this part, but he did not, staying up to stir and stir. The remaining ingredients were added in succession during the last two or three hours of cooking time. When I recently asked Debbie if her father might ever share his recipe with me, she e-mailed me right back, "Here's Daddy's recipe for a small black pot in the back yard." Mr. Gooch's recipe was short; just the list of ingredients. He figured people already knew how, and simply needed to know how much. I've added directions. Read it all the way through before you plan your stew, as it is an investment of time and attention, albeit one that yields worthy and satisfying results.

- 24 pounds hens
- 6 pounds stew beef
- 4 pounds dried limas
- 38 pounds potatoes
- 15 pounds onions
- 4 gallons tomatoes
- 1½ gallons cream white corn
- ¾ gallon whole white corn
- 1½ pounds fatback
- 3 pounds margarine
- Sugar, salt, black pepper, red pepper to taste
- Saltine crackers

1 This recipe requires one preparation day, and one cooking day. For stew preparation day, you will be working indoors, cooking the meat in batches and reserving both meat and broth, covered and chilled, overnight. You will need a 20-gallon-capacity outdoor stew pot, and a large food-safe wooden paddle for stirring the stew throughout the cooking time.

2 Working on an indoor stove, using stockpots and large Dutch ovens, cook the hens. If you can fit two into one pot with plenty of water over and around them, do so. Otherwise, one hen per pot. Bring each pot to a rolling boil over medium-high heat. Lower the heat to maintain an active simmer, and skim off and discard the foam as it rises, for 10 to 15 minutes. Then lower the heat again, to maintain a gentle but visible simmer, and cook for about 1 hour, until each hen is done. Transfer the cooked hens from their cooking pot to large platters, trays, or bowls, to cool to room temperature. Add more hens to the cooking pots and replenish the liquid with water so they are well covered.

3 As the hens cool down enough to handle them, begin separating and discarding the skin, bones, and gristle, and reserving the meat. Cover and chill the cooked chicken as you work, cooking the hens and preparing the meat. When all the hens are cooked, let the broth cool to room temperature and then cover and refrigerate it as well, until time to complete the stew.

4 Cook the beef in the same way, bringing it to a boil in water to cover it well, skimming away any foam, and then cooling, covering, and refrigerating both meat and broth until time to complete the stew.

5 Place the dried lima beans in big bowls with water to cover them by several inches and leave them to soak for 8 hours, or overnight. Set up a prep area for peeling and chopping the potatoes and onions on stew-cooking day.

6 On stew-cooking day, choose an outdoor spot where you can build a fire big enough to heat a large, cast-iron wash pot or another cooking vessel that can hold 20 gallons or more. You could use another outdoor heat source such as a powerful gas burner instead of a wood fire. You will need a big, long wooden paddle that you will use throughout the cooking process, to stir in all the ingredients, to help them break down as they simmer, and to keep the stew moving so that it does not stick to the bottom of the pot and burn.

7 Build a good, steady, slow fire in your chosen spot, and then place the pot over the wood fire or other outdoor cooking heat source. Pour in the reserved cooking broth from the beef and the chicken and let it heat up to a lively simmer. Add the beef and chicken and then add more water as needed, so that the pot contains lots of liquid, enough to generously cover the meat. Cook, stirring to keep the meat from sticking to the bottom of the pot or burning. →

8 Meanwhile, with someone always tending the pot and the fire outdoors, proceed with preparing the potatoes and onions. Peel and chop all the potatoes and all the onions into coarse chunks.

9 After the meat and broth have been simmering for about an hour, begin adding the potatoes and onions, stirring them in in batches. Continue stirring as these vegetables cook for 1 hour.

10 Then drain the soaked lima beans and add them to the pot. Continue cooking and stirring constantly for another hour, as the meat breaks down, the potatoes cook, and the onions soften.

11 After the stew has been cooking for about 2 hours, add the tomatoes and both kinds of corn. Continue cooking and stirring, adding more water to keep the stew well-nourished with cooking liquid and keep it from burning or sticking. Chop the fatback into four chunks and add it to the stew. Cook and stir for another 2 hours, making a total of about 6 hours of stewing time.

12 The stew should have thickened somewhat and become a handsome evenly red color, with potatoes, onions, tomatoes, and meat all breaking down and disappearing into the stew. Keep adding water to maintain a good moist consistency, even as the stew thickens up, and stir, stir, stir for another hour. When the stew is a pleasing thick texture, season it. First stir in the margarine, chopping it into big chunks and stirring it in to melt into the stew. (For the sugar, salt, and two kinds of pepper, Mr. Gooch leaves it up to us. I suggest you begin with ½ cup sugar and ½ cup salt, plus ¼ cup black pepper and 2 tablespoons red pepper flakes. After that, continue upping the seasonings until you find the ideal flavor for your stew.)

13 Let the fire die down, stirring all the while until the stew ceases to bubble and cook. Serve it hot with saltine crackers. Let leftover stew cool down to indoor room temperature. Transfer the stew to containers, seal each one airtight, and refrigerate for up to 3 days, or freeze for up to 3 months.

NOTE: *You can substitute for some ingredients in this recipe. For dried lima beans, you can use fresh or frozen lima beans or butterbeans. You can use either white or yellow creamed corn, and for the whole corn you can use white or yellow, canned, fresh, or frozen. For fatback, you can use bacon, thick or regular, cut into 1-inch pieces; you could use about 1 pound of some other smoky, fatty meat, or omit it altogether. You could use butter instead of margarine.*

Serves 25 to 30

Indoor Kitchen Burgoo

Arguments persist across state lines about the origins of Brunswick stew, with the states of Georgia and Virginia professing their claims with passion and earnest dedication, while North Carolina watches the ball being batted back and forth, high above its red clay soil. On the origins of burgoo, there is simply no dispute. Burgoo's homeplace then, now, and forevermore is the Bluegrass state of Kentucky. Nineteenth-century burgoo-fests drew thousands of people. Not only is burgoo the centerpiece of benefits and fundraisers throughout the year at church parish halls, community picnics, county fairs, and family gatherings, it is permanently on the menu at many a Kentucky restaurant or café. The town of Owensboro may or may not be where the stew originated, but it is surely the de facto home plate now. Barbecued mutton often shares top billing with burgoo at festivals and burgoo-centric celebrations. At home, you can serve burgoo with cornbread, yeast rolls, sliced white bread, or saltine crackers. Or stick with tradition and have a mutton barbecue sandwich, with slaw on the side.

- 2½ pounds chicken legs and thighs
- 1½ pounds boneless mutton or lamb, cut into large chunks
- 1½ pounds boneless beef, cut into large chunks
- 1 pound boneless pork, preferably Boston butt, country-style ribs, or chops, cut into large chunks
- Three 28-ounce cans whole peeled tomatoes
- 4 cups coarsely chopped potatoes
- 3 cups coarsely chopped onions
- 2 cups coarsely chopped cabbage
- 2 cups yellow or white corn, fresh, frozen, or canned
- 2 cups butterbeans or lima beans, fresh, frozen, or canned
- 1 cup coarsely chopped carrots
- 1 cup sliced fresh or frozen okra
- 1 cup chopped green bell pepper
- ¼ cup Worcestershire sauce
- 3 tablespoons coarsely chopped garlic
- 2 tablespoons salt
- 2 teaspoons freshly ground pepper
- 1 teaspoon dried red pepper flakes
- 1 cup chopped fresh parsley

1 In a large, heavy stockpot, combine the chicken, mutton, beef, and pork. Add enough water to cover the meats. Bring it to a rolling boil over high heat.

2 When the meat comes to a rolling boil, lower the heat to maintain an active boil, and begin to skim away any foam that rises to the top. Stir just enough to make sure the water can circulate around the various pieces of meat. Within 10 to 15 minutes, most of the foam will have risen to the top. Lower the heat to maintain a gentle but lively simmer and cook it for 2 to 3 hours, until the meat is very tender. You should be able to pull the various meats apart easily using two forks.

3 Remove the stockpot from the heat and set out a large deep bowl or baking pan, big enough to hold all the meat. Carefully transfer the meat to the bowl, leaving the broth behind in the stockpot. Spread the meat out so that it can cool down quickly. When the meat is cool enough to handle, remove and discard any bones and cartilage. Pull the meat apart into small pieces, using forks or your hands. You could also chop it coarsely. Return the meat to the stockpot and place it back on the stove.

4 Over very low heat, bring the meat back to a simmer. Meanwhile, add the tomatoes, potatoes, onions, cabbage, corn, butter beans, carrots, okra, bell pepper, Worcestershire, garlic, salt, pepper, and red pepper flakes. Stir the ingredients together. →

5 Increase the heat to medium-high and bring the stew back to a rolling boil. Stir well and then adjust the heat to maintain a lively, active simmer. Cook, stirring often, until the vegetables are tender, the meat has turned to shreds, and the burgoo has thickened into a chunky, rusty-red pleasing stew, 2 to 3 hours. Remove from the heat, sprinkle on the parsley, and serve the burgoo hot or warm.

NOTE: *For this recipe, bone-in meats work nicely and, in fact, add more flavor. Buy half again as much as the recipe requires, to allow for the weight of the bones. You can remove the bones at the same time as the chicken bones. Keep in mind that with a large stockpot full of stew, stirring gets more challenging toward the end of cooking time.*

There is little active cooking for this recipe, but since it needs a lively simmer in order to cook down, sticking and burning are possible. Adding water early on is fine, but toward the end, it could dilute the flavors. Your watchwords are "low and slow," but remember it needs to be visibly, actively cooking. Consider a two-day burgoo-cooking plan: You could cook the meats and make the broth on day one. Then let them cool overnight, and begin with boning and shredding on day two. Add the vegetables and cook it all down into burgoo.

Serves 4 to 6

Fried Quail with Cream Gravy

From Maryland down to Florida, and from West Virginia over to Texas, flocks of quail signal autumn's arrival. Hunters proudly share their takes, in farmhouse kitchens and elegant dining rooms alike. Southern fried or pan-sautéed; stuffed, roasted, or smothered; quail have long pleased both cooks and eaters, especially when accompanied by a luscious pan gravy. It extends quail's goodness, flavoring grits, rice, mashed potatoes, and dressing, while simply enhancing a hot-from-the-oven biscuit. Farm-raised quail are widely available today, and can be shipped anywhere in the country. Asian and Latino markets often carry them, whole or semi-boneless, meaning the leg-thigh portion and wings are left intact, while the rest is boned out for stuffing or pan-frying. Quail cook quickly and take to all manner of seasonings and sauces. *In The Taste of Country Cooking*, Edna Lewis reminisces about the bounty from the woods and fields around her family's land in Freetown, Virginia. She recalls quail as plentiful, often roasted with less-common game birds such as plover, snipe, woodcock, and squab. At about 4 ounces each for semi-boneless birds, two per person makes a pleasing main course. Serve this dish hot with rice, grits, or potatoes and a simple salad.

8 semi-boneless dressed quail
Salt
Freshly ground pepper
1 cup all-purpose flour, plus 2 tablespoons
About 1 cup vegetable oil
2 tablespoons butter
1½ cups milk

1 Season the quail generously on all sides with salt and pepper. Combine the 1 cup flour, 1½ teaspoons salt, and 1½ teaspoons pepper in a deep plate and mix well. Dredge each quail in the seasoned flour, turning to coat. Shake off extra flour and set aside on a clean plate.

2 Heat the vegetable oil and butter in a deep, 12-inch cast-iron skillet over medium heat until very hot. When the butter has melted and a pinch of flour sizzles at once, the fat is ready. Add the quail, breast-sides down, leaving some room between them. (Work in batches if need be, frying four quail at a time.) Cook undisturbed until handsomely browned, 3 to 4 minutes. Turn and fry until they have browned nicely and are tender and cooked through, 4 to 5 minutes more. Transfer the quail to a serving platter while you make the gravy.

3 Pour off most of the fat, leaving a good 2 tablespoons of the pan drippings in the skillet. Heat it until very hot and add the 2 tablespoons flour, stirring quickly to combine them evenly. Continue cooking, stirring constantly, until the flour has browned a little, just to an ivory shade, and thickened, 1 to 2 minutes.

4 Add the milk and stir to dissolve the flour mixture and start the gravy thickening. Let the gravy just come to a boil and then lower the heat. Add ½ teaspoon salt and ½ teaspoon pepper and stir well. Let it simmer, stirring often, until the gravy thickens into a smooth, luscious sauce, 3 to 5 minutes. (If the gravy becomes too thick, add a little more milk.) The gravy should be liquid and not pasty.

5 Remove the gravy from the heat, pour it over the quail, and serve them hot.

NOTE: *Cream gravy refers to a creamy, rich, white gravy made with drippings, flour, and milk rather than one made with cream or the more commonly used broth or water.*

Serves 6

My friend James McNair is the cookbook king—the person who revolutionized the cookbook world with his signature single-subject cookbooks, elegantly and practically designed, with gorgeous and inviting photographs of each dish. Beloved by readers and cooks, his books are rich with flavor and detail on each finite topic. James included this robust, satisfying wild duck dish from his Louisiana boyhood in his book *James McNair's Stews and Casseroles*. I asked him if I might include it here, along with its story, and he kindly obliged, saying "This is the way my mother always cooked the ducks shot by my daddy. Although I chose not to join in the hunt, much to Daddy's disappointment, I was always roped into helping pluck the pile of ducks that he'd bring home. Although the taste isn't quite the same, I've successfully made the dish here in California with domestic duck legs and thighs, which may not need to be cooked as long as their wild cousins. For several years now, however, my Napa Valley neighbor, who is an avid hunter, has shared his bounty of wild ducks, so I've been able to re-create the familiar long-ago flavor of my mother's gravy-smothered duck."

James McNair's Louisiana Duck Fricassee

- 5 to 6 pounds wild duck, bone-in, skin-on, cut into pieces, or domestic duck legs and thighs
- Salt
- Freshly ground pepper
- About ½ cup high-quality vegetable oil
- ¼ cup all-purpose flour
- 2 cups chopped onions
- 1 teaspoon minced or pressed garlic
- About 1½ cups Chicken Stock (page 152)
- 6 cups Everyday Rice (page 154)
- Minced green onions for garnish

1 Pat the duck dry with paper towels. Sprinkle it generously with salt and pepper.

2 Heat 3 tablespoons of the vegetable oil in a Dutch oven or other heavy stew pot over medium heat. Add as many of the duck pieces as will fit in the pot without crowding and brown them well on all sides. Transfer them to a plate. Brown the remaining duck in the same manner (there will probably be plenty of rendered fat from browning the first batch of duck, but if not, add more oil as necessary to prevent sticking).

3 Drain off all but ¼ cup of the drippings from browning the duck, saving any extra fat for another use. (If there's not enough rendered fat, add enough oil to the drippings to equal ¼ cup.) Add the flour to the drippings and cook the roux over medium heat, stirring almost constantly to prevent scorching, until it is dark brown, about 10 minutes. Add the onions and cook, stirring occasionally, until they are soft, about 10 minutes. Add the garlic and cook about 1 minute longer. →

4 Return the browned duck to the stew pot and add the chicken stock. Taste and adjust the seasonings. Bring the stock to a boil over medium-high heat, then turn the heat to low, cover tightly, and cook, stirring several times, until the duck is very tender when pierced with a small, sharp knife and the meat is almost falling off the bones, 1½ to 2 hours. (Stir in a little more stock, broth, or water if the gravy begins to thicken too much; it should remain the consistency of heavy cream.) Transfer the duck to a plate and keep the gravy warm.

5 When the duck is cool enough to handle, discard the skin and bones and shred or cut the meat into large chunks. Mound the rice in the center of a serving platter and place the duck around the edges. Pour the gravy over the top and sprinkle it with the green onions to serve.

NOTE: *At a local Asian supermarket, I found frozen birds known as "water ducks," which are quite slender compared to Pekin ducks and other farm-raised breeds that are the majority of available ducks in American stores. These ducks came with a tag identifying them as "Buddhist ducks," which means they are sold whole, plucked and dressed, but with the head and feet intact. I combined one water duck with several leg-and-thigh portions of domestic ducks to total 6 pounds. The results were spectacularly delicious.*

3

Shrimp *and* Crab, *the Beautiful Swimmers*

TECHNICALLY, THE LOVELY NAME "beautiful swimmers" refers only to crab. It comes from their scientific name, *Callinectes sapidus,* which combines Greek and Latin roots. The first part is Greek, with *calli* meaning "beautiful" and *nectes* meaning "swimmers." The second part, *sapidus,* means "savory," and that certainly fits as well. While *Callinectes sapidus* refers to only crab and not shrimp, I'm giving both species that accolade in my chapter title. I'm pairing them up unofficially because, to me, these two treasures of the cool blue ocean fit the description perfectly. Both are uniquely beautiful swimmers, and Southerners have been making savory dishes from them for longer than anyone can recall. We love both shrimp and crab, and with thousands of miles of coastline, we're blessed with seemingly endless options for places to find them for our tables.

Blue crabs skitter along the beaches and navigate the chilly waters of Maryland's Chesapeake Bay and down into Tidewater Virginia. North Carolina's coastal waters teem with plump gorgeous shrimp as well as blue crabs, and the shrimp- and crab-getting remains good all down the Atlantic coastline. Meandering along the Outer Banks of North Carolina, the Sea Islands, and Lowcountry of South Carolina and Georgia, looping around to Florida and circling around the Gulf of Mexico—there's so much water for fishing boats to ply with a plan, harvesting the beautiful swimmers for restaurants and seafood markets, near and far.

My first years of enjoying Southern shrimp meant feasting on them at fried-seafood places in Calabash and other beach towns like it, which pepper the coastlines of North Carolina and South Carolina. Fried in the mere whisper of seasoned flour, the seafood is dished up in a state both delicate and divine, with a pile of hushpuppies and slaw and plenty of tartar sauce on the side. I still love this meal, and I'm grateful so many other people do, too, keeping it easy to find all down the coast of both Carolinas, all year-round.

Despite this assembly of nine recipes for preparing shrimp and crab in various ways, keep in mind that we Southerners are perfectly content to cook either of these treasures simply by steaming or boiling them. Then, easily in the case of shrimp and with great care and patience in the case of crab, we open up or pull off their shells and enjoy the sweet, tender meat inside with simple accompaniments—including melted butter, lemon juice, sweet-and-tangy cocktail sauce, or that plain, mayonnaise-based condiment I love, tartar sauce. Here you'll find an array of dishes, from Chef Bill Smith's family favorite, hard-crab stew, to Charleston's signature she-crab soup, a simple take on shrimp and grits, a marvelous tomato-tinged etouffée, and a simple, crowd-pleasing, messy and spectacularly fun Lowcountry boil.

If you can get in the habit of packing away and freezing the shells when you peel raw shrimp, and then cooking up some shrimp stock (see page 153) when you have time, you will be glad you did. It takes a little organization, but what a benefit comes from your effort! A zip-top plastic freezer bag can be filled up over time, and in one stock-making session, you've got reddish-brown gold.

Serves 8

Lowcountry Seafood Boil

The Lowcountry begins along the southernmost coastal portion of North Carolina, extending through South Carolina and Georgia and on into the northernmost coastal areas of Florida. It includes the dozens of barrier islands dotting the coastline, which have been home to enslaved Africans and their descendants for more than two centuries. Gullah and Geechee cultures flourished here, and remain vibrant to this day, visible in terms of language, sweetgrass baskets, and culinary heritage, including the community-wide feasting known as a "Lowcountry Boil." From the start, West African cooks filled their traditional big iron pots with the Lowcountry's extraordinary seafood, particularly shrimp and clams. Modern-day seafood boils include corn on the cob, smoked sausage, and spices aplenty to flavor the feast. Wood fires have given way to gas burners, but these gigantic seafood extravaganzas still take place outdoors, and still abjure utensils in favor of hands-on eating. Crab, clams, and oysters; sweet potatoes and red potatoes—many ingredients extend the goodness in the pot. In northern Florida, it's called Land's End Stew, while South Carolina folks name it Beaufort Boil, Frogmore Stew, or Awendaw Seafood Pot.

- 3 tablespoons prepared shrimp boil, such as Old Bay Seasoning
- 3 tablespoons salt
- 2 pounds hot-smoked link sausage, cut into 2-inch pieces
- 12 ears freshly shucked corn, cut crosswise into 4-inch pieces
- 4 pounds medium shrimp, shell on
- Lemon or lime wedges for serving
- Melted butter for serving
- Hot pepper sauce for serving

1 Pour 4 quarts water into a large stockpot and place it over a gas burner or wood fire. Add the shrimp boil and salt. Bring it to a rolling boil over high heat.

2 Add the sausage, return the water to a boil, and cook for 5 minutes.

3 Add the corn and cook for 5 minutes, without waiting for the water to return to a boil.

4 Add the shrimp and cook for 3 minutes more, again without waiting for the water to reach a full boil.

5 Drain at once, turn out the pot onto a newspaper-covered table, and serve hot or warm with the lemon wedges, butter, and hot pepper sauce.

NOTE: *John Martin Taylor, author of* Hoppin' John's Lowcountry Cooking, *suggests a simple solution for putting the ingredients left over from a Lowcountry boil to good use: Combine peeled shrimp, corn cut off the cobs, and thinly sliced sausage in hot duck stock or tomato juice spiked with fresh hot chiles. Heat and enjoy!*

Serves 6 to 8

Creamy Shrimp Soup

When we're enjoying the sunny, sandy pleasures of vacationing at Holden Beach on the North Carolina coast, this simple soup puts the day's catch to work in a satisfying way. We hate to see the end of those hot, sun-drenched sandy days spent with my cousin Libbie and her family, but we do head back home with a wonderful souvenir: an ice-filled cooler of flavorful wild-caught shrimp. What a treasure to have handy in the freezer, so we can stir those summer memories into our soup bowls, warming up a wintry night! When you have an abundance of cooked shrimp on hand, whether purchased or left over from a recent shrimp boil, this soup makes a superb solution to the challenge of how to enjoy it. Finely chopping the shrimp in a food processor or blender releases their flavor, but if you don't have a machine handy, just leave them in big pieces and enjoy a chunky, delicious soup.

- 2 tablespoons all-purpose flour
- 1 teaspoon salt
- ½ teaspoon freshly ground pepper
- 1¼ pounds medium shrimp, in the shell
- 3 tablespoons butter
- 1 cup finely chopped celery
- ¾ cup finely chopped onion
- 2½ cups milk
- 3 tablespoons finely chopped green onions

1 In a 3-quart saucepan or Dutch oven, bring 1½ quarts water to a rolling boil over high heat. In a small bowl, combine the flour, salt, and pepper and stir with a fork to mix them well.

2 When the water reaches a lively boil, add the shrimp and stir. Cook just until they turn bright pink and become firm, 2 to 3 minutes. Scoop out the shrimp using a slotted spoon, leaving the water boiling. Rinse the shrimp briefly in cold water. Peel them, reserving the shells. Add the shells back to the simmering pot, and set the shrimp aside.

3 In a large skillet, melt the butter over medium-high heat. When it is sizzling and just beginning to brown, add the celery and onion and stir well. Cook, stirring often, until the celery brightens in color and the onion becomes fragrant, shiny, and softened, about 2 minutes.

4 Stir in the flour mixture and cook, stirring often, until the vegetables are evenly coated and the flour and butter begin to brown, 1 to 2 minutes more.

5 Scoop out the shrimp shells and discard them or strain the stock into a large bowl, and then return it to the pot. Scrape the celery mixture into the stock and stir well. While the soup simmers, chop each shrimp into three or four pieces. Add the chopped shrimp to the soup.

6 Increase the heat to medium-high and cook, stirring often, for 2 minutes. Add the milk and cook until the soup is evenly combined and thickened a little, 3 minutes more.

7 Stir in the green onions and cook, stirring occasionally, for 5 minutes. Working in batches, carefully transfer the soup to the bowl of a large food processor. Process until it is smooth, pulsing on and off and scraping down the sides as you go. You could also use an immersion blender or a standard blender by working in small batches. Allow steam to escape as you work with the hot soup and use the lowest speed to prevent splashing. Return the soup to the pot, bring it to a gentle boil, and serve it hot.

Serves 4 to 6

Shrimp Etouffée

Cajun French still seasons everyday conversations in southwest Louisiana, and French culture infuses the region's music, art, and cuisine. Centuries after French-speaking Canadians were expelled from Acadie, now Nova Scotia, and sought refuge in the bayous and prairies of southern Louisiana, their unique way of life endures. The word *étouffer* means "smothered or braised," and is a technique often used with crawfish, which come in season during the spring when rain floods the rice fields. Like gumbo, etouffée starts with a roux, but its color tends more toward warm brown than dark chocolate in tone, and it is often made with butter rather than oil or lard. Creole cooks make etouffée as well, and however much it may vary from Cajun to Creole and from cook to cook, one constant remains: serving it over a plate of hot rice. The sauce benefits greatly from the effort of making a little stock to amplify its crustacean goodness. Start your rice and then turn to your etouffée, which for all the beauty and goodness it brings you requires only a modest amount of energy and time in return.

- 1½ pounds head-on medium shrimp, or 1 pound medium shrimp, unshelled
- 1½ cups Shrimp Stock (page 153), Chicken Stock (page 152), or water
- 1 teaspoon dried thyme or 1 tablespoon fresh thyme
- 1 teaspoon salt
- ½ teaspoon freshly ground pepper
- ½ teaspoon cayenne pepper
- ½ teaspoon paprika
- 3 tablespoons butter
- 2 tablespoons all-purpose flour
- 1 cup chopped onion
- ½ cup chopped green bell pepper
- ½ cup chopped celery
- 1 tablespoon chopped garlic
- ¼ cup chopped green onions
- ¼ cup chopped fresh flat-leaf parsley
- Everyday Rice (page 154) for serving

1 Remove the shrimp shells, and heads if you have them, and place them in a medium saucepan. Cover and refrigerate the shrimp. Pour the stock over the shrimp shells and place the saucepan over medium-high heat. Bring it to a rolling boil, and then lower the heat to maintain a lively simmer. Cook for 20 minutes and then remove from the heat.

2 While the stock is simmering, stir the thyme, salt, pepper, cayenne, and paprika together in a small bowl, using a fork to combine them. When the stock is ready, pour it through a wire-mesh strainer into a measuring cup. Add a little water if needed to make 1½ cups.

3 Place a large heavy skillet or Dutch oven over medium-high heat and add the butter. Swirl to coat the pan as the butter melts. When a pinch of flour blooms on the surface when added to the butter, scatter in the flour and stir quickly and thoroughly, combining the butter and flour evenly into a thick, smooth roux. Continue cooking, stirring often, as the roux turns from white to golden brown, about 2 minutes. Add the onion, bell pepper, celery, and garlic and stir quickly, mixing the vegetables into the roux. Cook until everything is fragrant and softened, 1 to 2 minutes more.

4 Slowly add the stock, stirring and scraping to mix it in evenly. When the sauce is bubbling and boiling gently, lower the heat and cook, stirring now and then, until the sauce is thickened and smooth, about 15 minutes.

5 Scatter in the shrimp and let them cook undisturbed until the sides are turning visibly orange or pink, about 1 minute. Toss well and continue cooking, stirring often, until the shrimp are pink, firm, and cooked through and nicely flavored by the sauce. Add the green onions and parsley and stir well. Transfer the etouffée to a serving dish and serve it hot or warm over the rice.

Serves 4

Shrimp and Grits with Tomatoes and Bacon

When Craig Claiborne visited young, highly praised Southern chef and cookbook author Bill Neal at his Crook's Corner Restaurant in 1985, Neal served the *New York Times*'s emissary his signature version of shrimp and grits. Claiborne asked Neal to prepare this dish for him the following morning in his home kitchen, and included the recipe in his feature story on the chef. This moved a beloved Low-country dish from regional renown to a permanent place on the national culinary map. Given its vibrant colors, satisfying combination of textures, and flat-out deliciousness, that honor is richly deserved.

My version is a template you can adapt to suit yourself. Try smoked sausage, Cajun tasso, or ham, or make a meatless version using olive oil, fresh shiitakes, and arugula or baby spinach leaves. Either way, do enjoy the original Charleston dish, known as "breakfast shrimp." It's simply little fresh shrimp, ideally pulled from the shallow waters of a coastal inlet that very morning, quickly sautéed in a generous amount of butter and seasoned with pepper and salt. It is divine, even if you didn't net your own little catch. Start your grits first thing, then turn to cooking your shrimp.

- 4 bacon slices, chopped into ½-inch pieces
- ½ cup chopped onion
- 1 tablespoon chopped garlic
- 1 pound small to medium shrimp, shelled and deveined
- ¾ cup chopped fresh or canned tomatoes, with juice
- ½ cup loosely packed fresh basil or parsley
- 3 tablespoons thinly sliced green onions
- 1 teaspoon salt
- ½ teaspoon freshly ground pepper
- Everyday Grits (page 155) for serving

1 In a large, deep, heavy skillet over medium-high heat, cook the bacon, turning it often, until it curls up, browns handsomely, and releases its fragrance, 5 to 7 minutes. Scoop out the bacon onto a small plate and set it aside, leaving the grease in the pan.

2 Add the chopped onion to the same pan and cook, tossing it often, until it is fragrant, shiny, and tender, 2 to 3 minutes. Add the garlic and toss until it releases its fragrance, about 1 minute more.

3 Add the shrimp, scattering them around the pan and arranging them in a single layer. Cook them undisturbed until the sides are turning visibly orange or pink, 1 to 2 minutes, and then turn them over to cook the other sides until they are pink and becoming firm but not done, about 1 minute more.

4 Add the tomatoes and toss well. Lower the heat to maintain a gentle simmer and cook for 3 to 4 minutes while you prepare the basil leaves.

5 Reserving a sprig or two for garnish, press the remaining basil leaves into a mound and cut them into slender ribbons. Chop these in half crosswise and then fluff them with your fingers to separate the leaves again and return them to the cup measure.

6 When the shrimp are cooked and the tomato sauce has thickened just a bit, add the green onions, salt, pepper, and basil chiffonade and toss to mix everything together. Pour the hot grits out onto a large serving platter, mound the shrimp and tomatoes in the center, pour any remaining sauce over the top, and serve at once, garnished with the reserved basil.

Serves 6 to 8

Café Reconcile's White Beans with Shrimp

The great city of New Orleans abounds in fantastic, inviting places to dine, ranging from plain to fancy, inexpensive to luxurious, Creole to Cajun, and old-school to the next big thing. One I love to visit is Café Reconcile, a unique culinary destination dedicated to educating young people in the techniques and ingredients of the culinary profession. Since it opened in 2002 in the Central City neighborhood, Café Reconcile has trained thousands of young people in the culinary arts. Its graduates are now working in the hospitality industry in New Orleans and beyond. The ambience is as sunny as the window-filled corner dining room, and the menu features many classics such as this dish of great Northern beans simmered in a rich sauce with shrimp and herbs. This makes a generous pot of beans, which will taste even better the next day.

- 1 pound dried great Northern, navy, or baby white lima beans, soaked overnight and drained (see Note)
- 2 cups chopped onions
- 1 cup chopped celery
- 1 cup chopped green bell peppers
- ¼ cup chopped fresh flat-leaf parsley
- ¼ cup chopped garlic
- 1 tablespoon dried thyme or 2 tablespoons fresh thyme
- 1 teaspoon salt
- ½ teaspoon freshly ground black pepper
- ¼ teaspoon freshly ground white pepper
- ¼ teaspoon cayenne pepper
- 2½ quarts Chicken Stock (page 152) or water
- 1 tablespoon olive oil or vegetable oil
- 1½ pounds medium shrimp, peeled and deveined
- 2 cups cream, half-and-half, evaporated milk, or milk
- Everyday Rice (page 154) for serving

1 Place the beans in a Dutch oven or large pot. Add the onions, celery, bell peppers, parsley, half of the garlic, the thyme, salt, black pepper, white pepper, and cayenne. Add the stock and then bring it to a lively boil over medium-high heat.

2 Lower the heat to maintain a gentle but visible boil, and cook until the beans are very tender, about 2 hours. Skim off and discard any foam that rises early on in the cooking time.

3 Meanwhile, heat the olive oil in a large, heavy skillet over medium-high heat. Add the remaining garlic and cook, tossing it almost constantly, until it is shiny and fragrant but not browned, about 1 minute.

4 Add the shrimp to the skillet, scattering them around the pan and arranging them in a single layer. Cook them undisturbed until the sides are turning visibly orange or pink, 1 to 2 minutes, and then turn them over to cook the other sides until they are pink and becoming firm but not done, about 1 minute more.

5 Add the shrimp to the beans along with the cream. Stir to combine the shrimp with the beans and cook for 1 minute, taking care not to let the beans come back to a boil. Serve them hot or warm, with the rice.

NOTE: *If you want to make this now and can't wait for overnight soaking of the beans, use the quick-soak method. Place the beans in a large saucepan with enough cold water to cover them by 3 inches. Bring them to a rolling boil over high heat. Cook for 3 minutes and then remove from the heat. Let the beans stand for 1 hour; drain them well and proceed as directed.*

Serves 4

Buster Holmes's Crab Soup

Proprietor of a beloved neighborhood restaurant serving the New Orleans French Quarter from the 1940s through the early 1980s, Buster Holmes served up satisfying, delicious, affordable, and memorable Creole cooking so good that his name is remembered to this day. Famous for red beans and rice cooked with ham hocks, available as-is or with a pork chop or chicken on the side, Mr. Holmes ran an eatery where community and connection came free along with countless plates of lima beans, rabbit sauce piquante, shrimp Creole, or smothered chicken. Musicians stopped by for sustenance, and Mr. Holmes took his legendary red beans and rice up to Congo Square to please the music lovers gathered for the Jazz & Heritage Festival as long as he was able. Here is my version of Aunt Dump's Crab Soup, inspired by a recipe in his wonderful cookbook, *The Buster Holmes Restaurant Cookbook: New Orleans Handmade Cooking,* It's creamy and luscious, both elegant and simple to prepare.

- 2 teaspoons butter, at room temperature
- 2 teaspoons all-purpose flour
- ¾ cup cream, half-and-half, or evaporated milk
- 1 egg
- 3 cups milk
- ½ cup chopped onion
- ½ teaspoon salt
- ⅓ cup finely chopped fresh parsley
- 12 ounces cooked crabmeat
- 3 tablespoons finely chopped green onions

1 In a small bowl, combine the butter and flour and use a fork to mix and mash them into a smooth paste. In a medium bowl, combine the cream and egg. Using a fork, beat the egg into the cream, mixing them completely.

2 In a medium saucepan, combine the milk, onion, salt, and half the parsley; bring them to a gentle boil over medium-high heat. Add half the crabmeat, and stir well. Cook, stirring often, until the onion is fragrant and softened, about 3 minutes.

3 Stir the butter-flour paste into the saucepan. Continue cooking, stirring and pressing the paste against the sides of the pan to dissolve it into the soup.

4 Scoop out about ½ cup of the hot soup, and pour it slowly into the cream-egg mixture, stirring constantly to prevent the eggs from curdling. Repeat with another ½ cup soup, mixing them together quickly and well.

5 Pour the warmed cream-egg mixture back into the saucepan and stir in the remaining crab. Bring the soup to a gentle boil, and cook 1 minute more. Add the remaining parsley and the green onions, stir well, and serve the soup hot or warm.

Serves 6 to 8

William Deas's She-Crab Soup

Crabmeat, butter, cream, mace, and a splash of sherry make this luxurious, rich, yet delicate Charleston classic a special-occasion treat. This indulgent potage was the signature dish of William Deas, executive chef of Everett's Restaurant on Cannon Street, where he worked from the 1950s until his death in 1961. First published in 1930, the original soup recipe calls for an ingredient that's no longer commercially available: mature crab roe. Though female crabs caught in springtime may have immature roe hidden inside their shells, those with a she-crab's externally visible "sponge" of rust-colored eggs can no longer legally be taken. To protect the crab population, these "berried" she-crabs must be tossed back into the water at once. The recipe has always been seasonal, though, causing a 1950 version to offer cooks an off-season substitution: crumbling hard-boiled egg yolks into each soup bowl along with the sherry, before adding the soup. Twenty-first-century chefs sometimes use the immature roe from inside the crab, contributing some color and a textural richness. Frozen immature roe is available, as is flying fish roe, which resembles she-crab roe in color and texture. I love this soup just as it is, with the crab roe merely part of its history and a nod to dinners gone by.

- 1 tablespoon butter
- 3 tablespoons very finely chopped onion
- 1 teaspoon all-purpose flour
- 3½ cups milk
- ½ cup heavy cream, whipping cream, or half-and-half
- ¼ to ½ cup cooked crab roe (optional)
- 1 teaspoon Worcestershire sauce
- 1 teaspoon salt
- ½ teaspoon freshly ground pepper
- ¼ teaspoon ground mace (optional)
- 1½ cups cooked crabmeat
- 3 tablespoons dry sherry
- 2 tablespoons thinly sliced green onion
- 3 tablespoons finely chopped fresh parsley
- Dash of sweet or hot paprika
- ½ cup whipped cream (optional)

1 In a 3-quart heavy-bottomed saucepan or Dutch oven, melt the butter over medium heat. When it is foamy and a bit of onion sizzles at once, stir in the onion. Cook, stirring often, until the onion is shiny, softened, and fragrant, 1 to 2 minutes.

2 Sprinkle the flour over the onion and stir to mix it in. Cook, stirring occasionally, until the mixture is evenly combined, but not browned, 1 to 2 minutes more.

3 Add the milk, cream, crab roe (if using), Worcestershire, salt, pepper, and mace (if using). Stir to mix everything together. Cook, stirring now and then, while the mixture thickens and the flavors develop, about 15 minutes.

4 Add the crabmeat, sherry, and green onion and stir to mix them into the soup. Cook, stirring now and then, heating the crabmeat and allowing the flavors to develop for 2 minutes more.

5 Transfer the soup to a serving bowl, sprinkle it with the parsley and paprika, and serve it hot or warm, garnished with a dollop of whipped cream, if desired.

Serves 6 to 8

Ben and Karen Barker's Spicy Green Tomato Soup with Crab and Country Ham

Prior to 1986, when chefs Ben and Karen Barker opened Magnolia Grill in Durham, North Carolina, locals looking for a special-occasion dinner had a choice between steak houses and a few restaurants serving French-influenced food. From the beginning, the Barkers sought out local growers and food producers, giving the barely budding Carrboro Farmers' Market a strong assist as it got up and running. Like Alice Waters on the West Coast, the Barkers looked back to move forward, considering earlier culinary traditions with affectionate, thoughtful eyes. Magnolia Grill grew and prospered for more than two decades, inspiring dozens of chefs who worked for them to pursue their passions for Southern culinary excellence, and earning the Barkers numerous awards, including the highest honors from the James Beard Foundation. Their cookbooks continue to inspire home cooks with recipes like this lovely green, vibrant soup. Green unripe tomatoes fill the end-of-summer vines, calling for special treatment if they're to be used before frost shuts the gardens down. This signature soup, great cold as well as hot, is their savvy solution.

- ½ cup vegetable oil
- 5 ounces country ham or prosciutto, sliced into thin strips
- 2 cups thinly sliced onions
- 2 jalapeños, sliced, with seeds
- 4 green Anaheim chiles, seeded and sliced
- 2 green pasilla chiles, seeded and sliced
- 2 tablespoons chopped garlic
- 3½ pounds firm green tomatoes, cored and cut into eighths
- 1½ quarts Shrimp Stock (page 153) or Chicken Stock (page 152)
- 2 bay leaves
- 1 cup fresh basil leaves, plus more cut into chiffonade just before serving
- 3 tablespoons freshly squeezed lemon juice
- 1½ teaspoons hot sauce, such as Tabasco or Crystal
- 1 teaspoon salt
- 1 pound cooked crabmeat or shrimp, chopped into ¼-inch pieces
- 1 cup sour cream, thinned with 2 tablespoons milk
- 1 cup fresh tomato concassé (see Note) combined with ¼ cup capers, chopped
- ½ cup thinly sliced green onions

1 In a Dutch oven or large heavy saucepan, heat the vegetable oil over medium heat until hot. Scatter in the ham and cook, tossing often, until it is crisp and golden, 1 to 2 minutes. Transfer it to a small bowl and set it aside for garnishing the finished soup at serving time.

2 Add the sliced onions to the pan and cook, tossing often, until they are fragrant, shiny, and softened, 2 to 3 minutes. Add the jalapeños, Anaheim chiles, pasilla chiles, and garlic and cook, tossing often, until the chiles are fragrant, shiny, and softened, 4 to 5 minutes.

3 Add the tomatoes, stock, and bay leaves and bring the soup to a lively boil. Lower the heat to maintain a gentle but active simmer and cook, stirring often, until the tomatoes are very soft, 15 to 20 minutes. →

4 Remove the bay leaves, add the basil leaves, and remove the soup from the heat. Working in batches, transfer the hot soup to a blender and purée it until smooth. Season the soup with the lemon juice, hot sauce, and salt.

5 Divide the crab among individual soup bowls, mounding it in the center of each one. Ladle soup around the seafood, and garnish with swirls and dollops of the sour cream, dots or a cluster of tomato concassé, and a scattering of crisp country ham, basil chiffonade, and green onion. Serve immediately. Or let it cool to room temperature, cover and chill before garnishing, and serve cold.

NOTE: *For tomato concassé, drop fresh, ripe tomatoes into boiling water for about 30 seconds, just until you can easily peel them. Halve them crosswise, squeeze out and discard the seeds, and chop the tomatoes coarsely. You could substitute canned chopped tomatoes with juice for the tomato concassé.*

The Barkers occasionally made this dish with shrimp as well as with crab. The pink color of shrimp gives a lovely visual accent that crab can't match. While country ham is their porcine choice here, do try it with more easily found bacon or ham, if country ham isn't available.

Serves 10 to 12

Bill Smith's Hard-Crab Stew

My friend Bill Smith, a beloved and highly decorated chef of Crook's Corner in Chapel Hill, grew up in eastern North Carolina in the colonial-era town of New Bern. He remembers this particular dish as one his family enjoyed often but never at the dining room table. "My grandmother would make us go outside to eat it," he recalls. "The picnic table would be covered with newspaper and each place would be set with a nutcracker as well as silverware. After dinner, the shells would be rolled up in the newspaper and taken straight to the trash can." In the Outer Banks of North Carolina, cooks drop cornmeal dumplings around the stew's edges once it's simmering away, or layer in the flour dumplings known as "pie bread" among the crabs. For this one, you'll need to start with live blue crabs, cleaned by you or someone who loves or owes you, shortly before mealtime. For the porcine melody underlying this feast, salt-cured fatback or streak o' lean are the real deal, but thick-cut bacon is also delicious. On the issue of sliced white bread alongside, however, you'll get no grace from me. Grand-mother Smith used store-bought sliced white bread, so that's that. Bill Smith, ever gracious, shows mercy and allows that saltine crackers will work just fine.

- ½ pound sliced side meat or fatback, or thick-cut bacon
- 2 cups chopped onions
- 24 hard crabs, cleaned and halved (see Note)
- 4 bay leaves
- 1 teaspoon dried thyme or 1 tablespoon fresh thyme
- ½ teaspoon dried red pepper flakes
- 6 baking potatoes, peeled and cut into eighths
- ¾ cup cornmeal
- 1 teaspoon salt
- 1 teaspoon freshly ground pepper
- Sliced white bread or saltine crackers

1 Heat a large, heavy stockpot over medium heat until hot enough to make a bit of side meat sizzle at once. Render the fat from the meat by cooking it slowly, so that it releases its fat without smoking or burning. Cook, turning as often as needed, until the meat is handsomely browned, fragrant, and crisp, like well-cooked bacon, 7 to 9 minutes.

2 Transfer the meat to a plate and set it aside, leaving as much grease as possible in the stockpot. Scatter in the onions. Cook, stirring and tossing them often, until they are fragrant, shiny, and softened, but not browned, about 5 minutes.

3 Add the crabs, and then add cold water to cover the crabs by 2 inches. Stir in the bay leaves, thyme, and red pepper flakes. Break or coarsely chop the fried side meat into small pieces and add it to the pot as well.

4 Increase the heat to bring the water to a lively boil. Adjust to maintain an active, visible simmer, and let the stew cook for 30 minutes.

5 Add the potatoes and simmer until they are tender, 15 to 20 minutes more.

6 Increase the heat again to create a lively boil. In a small bowl, stir together 2 cups cold water and the cornmeal, then add it to the pot. Using a long-handled heatproof spoon, stir the stew to mix this in well, which will be a little awkward given that you are stirring around a whole mess of crab halves. Mix it in thoroughly, as best you can.

7 Let the stew come back to a lively boil as it begins to thicken. Add the salt and pepper and stir. Taste, and adjust the seasonings if needed. Cook until thickened and smooth, 2 minutes more.

8 Place two slices of white bread in the bottom of each large, individual serving bowl. Ladle stew generously over the bread, crabs and all. Guests will be picking the crabs apart with their hands, so offer nutcrackers or crab-claw crackers if you can, along with extra bread and plenty of napkins. Serve hot or warm.

NOTE: *In the best of all possible worlds, you will begin this fantastic stew with live crabs, which someone who thinks the world of you or this stew, or is professionally trained and compensated, will clean for you. This is referred to, oddly, as "dressing" them. Bill advises care and speed, as they will try to pinch you. You will need a big, heavy cleaver or butcher knife to whack each crab in two. Flip one crab over onto its back, slamming it down hard if possible so that it will be stunned and stop wiggling for a moment. Take aim and split the crab down the middle, between its claws, with one mighty whack or several determined whacks. Pop off both halves of the top carapace (shell) and rinse the crab well. Pull off and discard the soft, spongy, yellow-green gill filaments on the bottom, known as "devil's fingers." Bill thinks this name is a clue that they are not to be eaten. Set the crab aside and continue with the remaining crabs, stacking them in a large bowl or in a big baking pan. Perhaps your fishmonger will be able to perform these tasks shortly before you plan to begin your stew. If neither of these options works, Bill says that frozen dressed crabs make an acceptable hard-crab stew.*

4

Shellfish Stews, Fish Muddle, *and* Chowders

TAKE ONE LARGE COOKING POT; a generous supply of fish, clams, oysters, or mussels; a modest but flavorful hunk of salt pork; and an armful of potatoes and onions. Add water (which in olden times was often seawater), light the firewood, and you are on your way to a mighty fine and satisfying supper. Southerners have been making fish and shellfish soups forever, long before anyone thought to write about it. While there are standard ways we tend to approach the category, it's never been restricted by a sense of recipes or rules. The word *chowder* comes from the word *chaudière*, which is the French word for "cauldron," the massive, heavy-duty, cast-iron pot in which so many old-time stews were made. Another explanation is that it comes from *jowter*, an English term for a fishmonger or pescatory sales associate. Since Southerners were more likely to be catching their own or buying and trading at the docks rather than from a vendor in an English town, this seems a bit of a stretch. And who says that those jowters were cooks? Wherever it came from, the word *chowder* isn't widely used in the South compared to other parts of the United States. We're more likely to say plain old words like *soup*, *stew*, or the lovely English term *muddle*, meaning "a jumble, a mess, or a disorganized assembly of things."

Whatever the term, the stews are often rather carefully layered into a pot with salt pork, sliced onions, sliced potatoes, whole or cut-up fish, and sometimes eggs. Southerners have just one main chowder, from North Carolina's Outer Banks, made with clams or saltwater fish. My old-school version, which is simple, satisfying, and oceanically delightful, contains no cream, no milk, no butter, and no flour. Nothing but potatoes, onions, and salt pork to help the shellfish carry the day.

Along the Atlantic coastline, oysters have a Christmas association in the South, since mid- to late December was the consensus of when it was absolutely positively cold enough outside, all the way inland to the Piedmont and beyond, to safely pack them up in barrels and ship them inland from ports like Charleston, Savannah, and Wilmington, North Carolina. Citrus fruits and coconuts came into season from tropical climes around the winter holidays. This gave them a holiday cachet for ambrosia and coconut cakes, to be served with the Christmas Eve oyster stew, which I remember my grandfather making when I was very small.

In this chapter, you'll find fish stews made with catfish, channel bass or rockfish, and red drum; clams cooked in gravy, Geechee- and Gullah-style; that simple, superb clam chowder beloved along the barrier islands in North Carolina's Outer Banks; and two variations on an oyster stew theme, one easygoing weeknight style and one for special nights at home. You may find from this chapter that fish and shellfish become your favorite dish!

Serves 4 to 6

Granddaddy's Oyster Stew

My maternal grandfather spent plenty of time in the kitchen on the dairy farm where he and my grandmother had raised their daughters and still worked 'til I was grown. His activities therein had one purpose only: eating, rather than cooking, canning, preserving, or cleaning. One exception was Christmas Eve, on which night Granddaddy stepped up to the kitchen counter and stove and orchestrated the making of this simple soup. Nothing to it but milk, butter, salt, and pepper, creating a simple elegant liquid stage on which just-shucked oysters fresh from the North Carolina coast got to dance. The name "soup" fits better than "stew," given the dish's milk-not-cream base and its minuscule cooking time of under ten minutes. You may spend more time eating it than you do cooking it, not that you would need speed as a reason to make this. You know that its name, despite its description, is simply stew. Oyster Stew. We love making it and eating it on cold, wintry evenings. Wait for Christmas? No way! This lovely dish needs no occasion. Only wonderful fresh oysters, soft butter, and a sleeve of saltine crackers.

1 quart milk

12 ounces shucked fresh oysters, with liquid

1 teaspoon salt

1 teaspoon freshly ground pepper

3 tablespoons butter, cut into chunks

Saltine crackers for serving

1 In a 2-quart saucepan, heat the milk over medium heat until it just reaches a gentle boil. Stir in the oysters and all their liquid.

2 Cook just until the oysters begin to curl around the edges, 2 to 4 minutes. Add the salt and pepper and stir well. Add the chunks of butter and stir to melt.

3 Ladle the stew into serving bowls and serve it at once, passing the crackers.

Serves 6

French Quarter Oyster Stew

New Orleans knows how to celebrate, and while some might find the Big Easy's ways excessive, I share the city's appreciation for layering luxurious ingredients and extending the pleasure of a feast by kicking it off in a grand way. The tradition of elegant oyster stew in puff pastry shells as a first course on Thanksgiving epitomizes this approach, and while I wouldn't limit this dish to once a year, I think it makes beautiful sense. Briny, glistening oysters, onions, celery, a kiss of butter, and an adulation of cream? What could be more glorious to those of us who find oysters irresistible in every form? My version of the kind of oyster stew served at Antoine's and other French Quarter palaces of dining is simply made and gratefully received, first course to a feast or supper in a bowl. You can prepare the soup up until the point where you add the milk, cream, and oysters, and set that aside until just a few minutes before serving time. Puff pastry cases are optional, but do have some hot French bread, rolls, or biscuits for dipping up the last drops of oyster stew.

- ⅔ cup oyster liquor, fish stock, or bottled clam juice
- 12 ounces shucked fresh oysters, with liquid
- 6 tablespoons butter
- 3 tablespoons all-purpose flour
- 1 cup finely chopped celery
- 1 cup finely chopped onion
- ¼ cup finely chopped fresh flat-leaf parsley
- 2 teaspoons finely chopped garlic
- 1 teaspoon salt
- ¾ teaspoon freshly ground pepper
- ¼ teaspoon cayenne pepper
- 1½ cups milk
- 1 cup heavy cream

1 Combine the oyster liquor with 1 cup water in a 4-quart saucepan. Bring it to a simmer over medium heat. Add the oysters and their liquid and simmer, gently shaking the pan to heat them evenly, until they just begin to curl around the edges, about 2 minutes. Using a slotted spoon, scoop out the oysters into a medium bowl; pour the cooking liquid into a pitcher or bowl, and set both aside.

2 Heat the butter in the same saucepan over medium-high heat. When a pinch of flour blooms on the surface when added to the butter, scatter in the flour and stir quickly and thoroughly, combining the butter and flour evenly into a thick, smooth roux. Continue cooking, stirring often, as the roux turns from white to golden brown, 3 to 4 minutes.

3 Turn the heat to medium and add the celery, onion, parsley, garlic, salt, pepper, and cayenne. Cook, stirring frequently with a wooden spoon, until the onion and celery are very soft, about 25 minutes.

4 Stir in the milk, cream, oysters, and reserved cooking liquid. Cook, stirring occasionally, until they're just hot, about 5 minutes. Serve the stew immediately.

Serves 4 to 6

Pine Bark Stew

People in Darlington County, South Carolina, take pride in this stew of freshwater fish simmered with salt pork and onions in a tomato-enriched broth. Locals trace its origins to Pee Dee River fishing camps, where abundant catches of catfish, rockfish, blue bream, bass, or trout inspired folks to devise a good way to put said fish to use. North Carolina and Georgia cooks make this dish as well, and nobody is certain how far back it goes, though early-twentieth-century roots are clear. Efforts to explain the oddball name are extremely creative and suspect. Could the stew have been so thick people ate it off sections of pine bark, which tends to be rather crumbly? Was it cooked over a fire made of pine bark? Maybe so, given the region's abundance of pine trees, but surely other dishes simmered on the same fuel, so why the name for this one? Could seasonings really have been so scarce that cooks stirred pine tree bark or roots into the stew? My vote is this: Let us embrace the mystery! Nobody knows, nothing makes sense, and while guessing passes the time, I'm satisfied with the fact that this makes a pleasing stew that pairs with saltine crackers, cornbread, or biscuits.

- 6 thick-cut bacon slices, cut into ½-inch pieces
- 2 cups diced potatoes
- 1 cup chopped onion
- 1 teaspoon dried thyme or 1 tablespoon fresh thyme
- 1 teaspoon salt
- 1 teaspoon freshly ground pepper
- ½ teaspoon cayenne pepper
- 2 pounds firm freshwater fish fillets, such as catfish, rockfish, trout, or perch
- 5 cups boiling water
- 1½ cups peeled whole plum tomatoes, chopped, with juice
- ¼ cup finely chopped green onions
- ¼ cup chopped fresh flat-leaf parsley

1 Heat a Dutch oven or a large saucepan over medium heat until hot. Cook the bacon, turning often, until it curls up and becomes crisp, fragrant, and nicely browned. Scoop the bacon out and set it aside on a plate, leaving the grease in the pan.

2 Add the potatoes to the same pan and cook, tossing them often, for 2 minutes. Add the chopped onion and continue cooking, tossing often, until fragrant and softened, 2 minutes more. Add the thyme, salt, pepper, and cayenne and toss to mix everything together. Spread the onion and potatoes out into an even layer covering the bottom of the pan.

3 Carefully place the fish fillets on top of the cooked potatoes and onion. Pour the boiling water over the fish slowly, to avoid disturbing the fillets.

4 Let the water come back to a boil and then adjust the heat to maintain a gentle simmer, until the fish is cooked through and the vegetables have flavored the broth, about 30 minutes.

5 Add the tomatoes and stir well. Cook, stirring gently and carefully, for 10 minutes more. When the fish is flaky and the potatoes are tender, stir in the bacon and remove the stew from the heat. Serve it hot, garnished with the green onions and parsley.

Serves 10 to 12

Outer Banks Old Drum Stew

Officially designated as the North Carolina State Saltwater Fish in 1971, red drum thrive in the mid-Atlantic coastal waters. To Outer Banks residents, known as "bankers," red drum mean two things: Autumn is here, and it's time to cook Old Drum Stew. Also called channel bass, red drum can live forty to sixty years, growing too large for a single family's supper. When they are caught, bankers either salt and dry them, or make this stew for family, neighbors, and friends. Mostly this is a community cooking effort, but a few restaurants serve Old Drum Stew as a weekly special during the autumn season. Kitchen crews divide up the tasks: peeling and cooking the potatoes, chopping and frying up the fatback, boiling eggs, and preparing the fish. None of it is difficult, but it does take time, with many hands working toward a delicious goal. Not everyone agrees on the fine points, though. The onions could be cooked, or left raw. The eggs are hard-boiled, but they could be sliced, chopped, or left whole. The meat could be fatback or streak o' lean. Cornbread is standard, but cornmeal dumplings dropped into the pot to simmer are a beloved alternative.

- 2 pounds red potatoes, cut into 3-inch chunks
- 3 pounds red drum or channel bass fillets, cut into 2-inch cubes
- 4 teaspoons salt
- 1 pound fatback, side meat, streak o' lean, or thick-cut bacon, cut into 1-inch pieces
- 2 cups chopped onions
- 10 hard-boiled eggs, peeled and cut into ½-inch slices
- Hot Skillet Cornbread (page 159) with butter for serving

1 Set out two large saucepans for cooking the potatoes and the fish. Place the potatoes in one and the fish in the other. Fill each with water to cover by 2 inches, and add 2 teaspoons of the salt to each pot. Set out a large, heavy skillet, preferably cast-iron, for cooking the fatback.

2 Place the pots of potatoes and fish on the stove over medium-high heat and let each one come to a lively, active boil. Adjust the heat to maintain a gentle boil and cook until the fish are just flaky and the potatoes are fork tender, 10 to 15 minutes for each pot. Check early and often, so as not to overcook either one.

3 When the fish and potatoes are ready, drain off the water, cover the pots with a lid or a plate, and set both pots aside on the back of the stove to keep warm.

4 Cook the fatback, scattering it in the heavy skillet over medium-high heat. Let the meat brown and render its fat, tossing and turning as needed and allowing it to color nicely and become crisp. When the meat is handsomely browned and crispy, scoop it out into a bowl and cover to keep it warm. Pour the grease into another bowl and cover it to keep it warm as well.

5 Set out large plates for each guest and arrange big bowls or platters for each component of this meal: cooked drum, cooked potatoes, chopped onions, crisp fatback (also known as "cracklins"), hot fatback grease, sliced hard-boiled eggs, and hot cornbread with butter.

6 Invite each guest to serve out a good portion of fish and potatoes, then add a sprinkling of chopped onion and fried fatback. Spoon or pour some of the hot grease over the top and place sliced hard-boiled eggs on the side. Serve it hot or warm, inviting your guests to mash their potatoes and fish together and eat them along with the accompaniments.

Serves 8

Fred Thompson's Carolina Seafood Muddle

All along the North Carolina coastline, and up through the sounds and inlets where saltwater and freshwater meet, countless species of fish and seafood thrive. This abundance has kept home cooks, families, and community groups busy for too many years to count, hauling in the day's or season's best catch and getting it to the table. Fred Thompson grew up in Johnston County, North Carolina, closer to Raleigh and the Piedmont than to the Outer Banks, but years of fishing trips and research for his numerous cookbooks have made him an honorary "banker." Fred loves to stir up a muddle—a big mess of seafood cooked in a great cauldron over glowing coals. I'm so glad he translated his rustic muddle into a stovetop iteration, with saltwater flavor and the traditional garnish of hard-boiled eggs. Stock up on saltine crackers to go along with your muddle, or serve Skillet Cornbread (page 159) with lots of butter.

- ½ pound sliced thick-cut bacon
- 2½ cups chopped onions
- 1 tablespoon chopped garlic
- 3 cups chopped tomatoes, with juice
- 3 cups peeled, thinly sliced red potatoes
- 2 cups bottled clam juice
- 2 tablespoons apple cider vinegar or white vinegar
- 1 teaspoon dried thyme or 1 tablespoon fresh thyme
- 1 teaspoon salt
- 1 teaspoon freshly ground pepper
- 1 teaspoon dried red pepper flakes
- 1½ pounds snapper, halibut, grouper, bass, or cod, cut into 1½-inch chunks
- 1 pound medium shrimp, peeled and deveined
- ½ pound bay scallops
- 8 eggs
- ¼ cup thinly sliced green onions
- ¼ cup chopped fresh flat-leaf parsley

1 In a Dutch oven or a large, heavy pot, cook the bacon until it is crisp and nicely browned, turning it often. Leaving the grease in the pot, transfer the bacon to a plate to cool, and then crumble or chop it into small pieces.

2 Heat the pot over medium-high heat and add the chopped onions. Toss them and cook until they are fragrant, shiny, and softened, 2 to 3 minutes. Add the garlic and toss it well.

3 Add the tomatoes, potatoes, clam juice, vinegar, and 3 cups water and stir them together. Add the thyme, salt, pepper, and red pepper flakes. Let the muddle come to a lively boil, and then adjust the heat to maintain a visible simmer. Cover and cook, stirring it once or twice, until the potatoes are tender, 15 to 20 minutes.

4 Add the fish, placing it in a single layer on top of the vegetables. Place the shrimp all over the stew, and scatter in the bay scallops as well. Then add water as needed to just cover the fish, but not the shrimp. Cover and cook it undisturbed, until the fish are opaque and flaky and the shrimp are bright pink, 3 to 4 minutes.

5 Meanwhile, crack four of the eggs into small bowls. When the shrimp are pink, uncover the muddle, and gently slide the eggs in on the surface of the soup, one by one, placing them evenly around the edges of the pot. Repeat with the remaining four eggs, and then cover and cook them for 1½ to 2 minutes. Scoop a little soup stock over the poaching eggs. Scatter the reserved bacon, green onions, and parsley over the soup. When the eggs are poached, quickly scoop them out into individual serving bowls. Ladle out the seafood muddle over the eggs, making sure each bowl gets beautiful chunks of fish, bright pink shrimp, and little scallops. Serve hot or warm.

Serves 4 to 6

Carolina Clam Chowder, Down-East Style

Once you've passed through North Carolina's capital city of Raleigh en route to the coast, you find yourself in the vast region known as "Down East." The red clay soil gets sandy, the pine trees grow taller, and the highways flatten out. A few hours takes you to the coastline, which forms an undulating chain of slender islands, curving and bending to enclose the Pamlico Sound. The sound and Inland Waterway it feeds teem with boats, while the Atlantic Ocean churns with marine life, pelicans, swans, and wild geese. People who live in communities on or near the Outer Banks call themselves "bankers," and share a love and respect for nature in their landscape, which is unlike any other place on Earth. Seafood restaurants abound, with fancy versions of clam chowder among their offerings, but none beats this homespun version, sans cream, sans razzmatazz. Nothing to it—"nothing" being a few worthy items: chewy, flavor-packed clams; potatoes; onions; and a handful of bacon. Minutes of minor effort, and you've created a simple feast. Saltine crackers go nicely with this, though Skillet Cornbread (see page 159) would fit right in.

- 36 to 48 small clams, such as littlenecks, or 24 large clams, enough to yield about 1 cup of clam meat
- 6 ounces thick smoky bacon, finely chopped
- 1 cup finely chopped onion
- 1½ cups peeled chopped red or white potatoes
- ½ teaspoon salt
- ½ teaspoon freshly ground pepper

1 Rinse the clams well and place them in a stockpot with about 2 cups water. Cover and bring them to a rolling boil. Cook just until the clams open, 3 to 5 minutes. Remove them from the heat, transfer the clams to a plate or bowl, discarding any that do not open, and let them cool, reserving all the cooking liquid.

2 When the shells are cool enough to handle, remove the clam meat and reserve. (If you used larger clams, chop the clam meat coarsely so that it's easy to eat with a spoon.) Strain the liquid, discarding the shells, and reserve it alongside the clams.

3 In a medium saucepan over medium heat, cook the bacon until it is nicely browned and aromatic, about 3 minutes. Scoop out the bacon and set it aside, reserving the grease in the pan.

4 Add the onion and cook, stirring often, until fragrant and shiny, but not browned, about 5 minutes. Add the potatoes, bacon, salt, pepper, and reserved clam cooking liquid, along with 2½ cups water. Simmer over medium-high heat for about 20 minutes, or until the potatoes are tender. Add the clams back into the pot and cook just enough to heat them through, about 1 minute more. Serve the chowder hot or warm.

Serves 4

Cornelia Walker Bailey's Geechee Clams in Gravy

Cornelia Walker Bailey is the guardian angel of Sapelo Island, one jewel in the geographical necklace known as the Sea Islands, just off the coastlines of South Carolina and Georgia. This island is home to descendants of the West African people who arrived enslaved and survived to make it their home. Mrs. Bailey's memoir, *God, Dr. Buzzard, and the Bolito Man: A Saltwater Geechee Talks about Life on Sapelo Island, Georgia*, cookbook, and community work nourish Saltwater Geechee culture on Sapelo today.

She explains this recipe best: "I love this in the morning, served over grits with biscuits and butter and a hot cup of coffee!" Adding parsley and green onions would be acceptable, she told me, ". . . but don't dress it up too much. We don't camouflage it with a lot of stuff. We let that clam speak for itself! All you need are smoked bacon, onions, not a bunch of things. Salt, pepper, sugar, onions, and bacon were the only seasonings we had. We get hardshell clams out of the water, out of the mud banks and the sands around Sapelo Island. You cook the roux to the color you want the final gravy to be. Clams are gray, and you're putting it over grits or rice, which are white, so you want a nice caramel color. Take your time for a brown you can see!"

- 1 tablespoon vegetable oil
- ⅓ cup chopped bacon
- ½ cup coarsely chopped onion
- 3 tablespoons all-purpose flour
- 1 to 2 cups chopped clam meat, fresh (see Note), frozen, or canned, reserving 1 cup liquid or juice (or use bottled clam juice or fish stock)
- 2 tablespoons thinly sliced green onions
- 2 tablespoons chopped fresh flat-leaf parsley
- Everyday Grits (page 155) or Everyday Rice (page 154) for serving

1 In a large, heavy skillet, heat the vegetable oil over medium-high heat until a bit of bacon sizzles at once. Scatter in the chopped bacon and cook it undisturbed as it sizzles and begins to curl up and brown on one side. Toss it well, and stir to separate it into pieces and cook it evenly. When the bacon is fragrant and barely browned, add the onion and toss them together. Continue cooking, stirring and scraping while the onion softens.

2 When the onion is shiny and fragrant, scoop the onion and the bacon out onto a small plate, leaving behind as much of the oil as possible. Leave the skillet over medium-high heat.

3 When a pinch of flour blooms on the surface when added to the oil, scatter in the flour and stir quickly and thoroughly, combining the oil and flour evenly into a thick, smooth roux. Continue cooking, stirring often, as the roux turns from white to a light golden color, about 2 minutes. (Take care and add more oil if needed to keep it from sticking.)

4 Add the reserved clam juice and 1 cup water and stir them into the roux. Add the cooked onion and bacon along with the clams. Bring them to a boil, lower the heat to maintain a gentle but visible simmer, and cook until thickened, about 10 minutes.

5 Stir in the green onions and parsley. Serve the clams hot or warm, over the grits.

NOTE: *For fresh clams, you will need about 24 small clams, such as cherrystone, littleneck, or top neck clams. Rinse them well in cool running water. Using a clam knife or oyster knife or a standard table knife, and working over a large bowl, open each clam, taking care to reserve the liquid inside as you work. You could also briefly cook the clams in a small amount of water in a covered pot. Place them over high heat and cook just until the water boils and the clams open wide. Reserve all the cooking liquid to use in your recipe, as it will include clam juices and be delicious. You could also put the clams in the freezer for 2 hours or so, until they open and partially freeze. Scrape out all the meat and transfer it to a small bowl. Once you have opened the clams, strain their juice well through a wire-mesh strainer into a measuring cup. Add water or clam juice to make 2 cups.*

5 Hearty Bowls *of* Chicken, Beef, *and* Pork

WHETHER COOKING OUTDOORS in an enormous cast-iron wash pot over an open fire, or tending a big Dutch oven on an electric stove in a cozy kitchen, Southern cooks have a history of stretching meat into thrifty and pleasing meals. Whether that protein source was meat they had caught, hunted, raised, or purchased, Southerners learned to turn it into robust, satisfying soups and stews. One fried chicken meant a special treat for company at Sunday dinner, but everybody knew to fill up on the biscuits, macaroni and cheese, field peas, deviled eggs, candied yams, and mashed potatoes and gravy because unless you owned a lot of chickens, no one expected more than one piece. That same chicken, however, stewed together with lima beans, corn, tomatoes, and potatoes, or simmered in its own broth with some rice could satisfy an entire extended family with seconds to go around. This chapter is a feast of hearty, everyday dishes, from chicken bog and jambalaya to beefy Big Easy–style ya-ka-mein noodles and cold-weather-curing, vegetable-packed, comforting ham-bone soup. From South Carolina's Pee Dee River basin to Cajun country, and from Daufuskie Island to Pensacola and down to Little Havana, this chapter serves up fantastic solutions to the problem of feeding lots of people lots of food, wonderfully well.

Serves 6 to 8

Jay Pierce's Chicken Stew with Lima Beans

At Rock Salt in Charlotte, North Carolina, Chef Jay Pierce's spirited seasonal menus put a twenty-first-century spin on traditional ingredients and dishes. At home with his family, he cooks dishes like Granny's stew, a roux-based old-school pot of goodness from his Louisiana childhood. Jay's grandmother, Esma Richoux Trosclair, was not one to measure, nor is Jay's mom, who makes it in Granny's 12-quart Magnalite pot; fortunately Jay watched her and wrote it down. "First you make a roux . . . " applies here, which Jay notes is for flavor even more than for its thickening and coloring properties. Burn that roux? Worst thing you could do, Jay recalls, because that would be wasting food. The dish started out as a variation on etouffée, since a shellfish allergy kept Granny from eating that. Back in Marrero, Louisiana, just across and up the river from New Orleans, Granny cooked her stew with whole chicken and served it with the bones left in. Jay's mom uses chicken cut into pieces, removing the bones and skin toward the end. Both season this stew with Tony Chachere's Creole Seasoning and you can, too, using a generous tablespoon of Tony's in place of the salt and the black and cayenne peppers.

¾ cup vegetable oil
¾ cup all-purpose flour
1¼ cups chopped onions
¾ cup chopped green bell pepper
¾ cup chopped celery
1 tablespoon finely chopped garlic
3¾ pounds bone-in, skin-on chicken, preferably a whole chicken cut into serving pieces
2 cups Chicken Stock (page 152)
2 teaspoons salt
1 teaspoon freshly ground pepper
1 teaspoon cayenne pepper or dried red chili flakes
1 teaspoon dried thyme, or about 5 sprigs fresh thyme
4 bay leaves
3 cups butterbeans or lima beans, fresh, frozen, or canned
⅓ cup chopped fresh flat-leaf parsley

1 Heat the vegetable oil over medium heat in a large, heavy skillet, such as cast iron, until hot. When a pinch of flour blooms on the surface when added to the oil, scatter in the flour and stir quickly and thoroughly, combining the oil and flour evenly into a thick, smooth roux. Continue cooking, stirring often, as the roux turns from white to ivory to a rich, medium brown, the color of peanut butter. This will take 30 minutes or so, and your dedication will be rewarded by the fine deep flavor you are creating so patiently.

2 Scatter in the onions, bell pepper, celery, and garlic and stir well. Mix them in quickly, to coat them with the roux and prevent it from darkening any further. Toss them and remove the pan from the heat.

3 When the vegetables stop sizzling, transfer them to a Dutch oven or other large cooking pot. Heat the roux over medium-high heat, and as soon as it is sizzling, add the chicken pieces, a few at a time. Turn to season them with the roux as they begin to brown. When all the chicken is in the pot, add the stock and 1 cup water and bring them to a gentle boil.

4 Combine the salt, pepper, cayenne, thyme, and bay leaves in a small bowl and stir them with a fork to mix them together. Stir the spice mixture into the chicken pot. When the stew comes to a lively boil and the roux has dissolved into the sauce, lower the heat to maintain a gentle but visible simmer and cook, stirring often, until the sauce is pleasingly thick and the chicken is tender and cooked through, about 1 hour.

5 If you want to remove the bones, turn the heat to very low and transfer the chicken pieces to a large platter or a big bowl, using tongs or a large spoon. Use two forks to separate the meat from the bones. Add the meat back to the pot and discard the bones and gristle. Scrape any sauce remaining on the platter back into the pot.

6 Let the stew come back to a lively boil and add the butterbeans. If using fresh or frozen butterbeans, cook until they are tender, 5 to 10 minutes. If using canned butterbeans, cook just until they are heated through and coated with the sauce. Add the parsley, stir well, and serve the stew hot or warm.

If you ask people where the action is in Horry County, South Carolina, most of the year, they will point you in the direction of the bustling city of Myrtle Beach. If it's the third weekend in October, though, get them to show you the way to Loris, twenty miles inland and home of the Annual Loris Bog-Off. Gigantic cast-iron cauldrons and shiny stockpots bubble away, filled with a simple, supremely delicious stew of chicken, onions, smoked sausage, and long-grain rice, simmered into the satisfying stew known as chicken bog. But why is it so named? Because it's moist and boggy? Because the chicken gets all bogged down in the rice-and-broth goodness? Nobody knows, nor much cares, providing they receive a generous serving. Chicken bog belongs in the great South Carolina family of dishes known as *pilau* and *perloo*, meaty rice-centered main dishes with ancient Persian and South Asian roots. It anchors fund-raisers, family reunions, victory celebrations, and cooking contests such as the one at the Robeson County Fair up across the state line in Lumberton, North Carolina. They've been celebrating the bog-off in Loris since 1979, because as good as chicken bog is to eat, it's as much fun to make it outdoors every October.

Serves 6 to 8

Chicken Bog

- 1 chicken (about 3½ pounds), whole or cut in serving pieces
- 8 ounces smoked sausage such as kielbasa or andouille, halved lengthwise and cut crosswise into ½-inch pieces
- 1½ cups long-grain rice
- 1 cup chopped onion
- 1 teaspoon salt
- 1 teaspoon freshly ground pepper
- 2 tablespoons butter

1 Place the chicken in a large Dutch oven or stockpot and add enough water to cover it by 2 inches. Bring it to a rolling boil over medium-high heat. Skim off and discard any foam that rises to the surface. After 10 minutes, when the foam has subsided, lower the heat to maintain a gentle but visible simmer. Cook until the chicken is tender and done to the bone, 45 minutes to 1 hour.

2 Transfer the chicken to a platter or baking pan until it is cool enough to handle. Leave the pot of chicken broth on the stove. When the meat has cooled, pull it from the bones and set it aside, discarding the skin and bones. For the traditional bog, leave the chicken in large chunks. If you wish, chop it into big bite-size pieces.

3 Measure the chicken broth. You should have 6 cups. Add water if needed to make that amount. Return the broth to the cooking pot and add the chicken meat, sausage, rice, onion, salt, and pepper. Place the pot over medium-high heat and bring it to a lively boil.

4 Turn the heat to low and stir once to mix everything together. Continue cooking without stirring, until the rice has absorbed most of the liquid but is still moist, shiny, and tender, 30 to 35 minutes.

5 Remove the pot from heat, add the butter, and stir gently to mix everything together well. Let the bog stand 10 or 15 minutes if possible, to let the flavors settle, and then serve it hot or warm.

Serves 12 to 14

James Naquin's Chicken and Sausage Jambalaya

My friend James Naquin celebrates his birthday by inviting dozens of friends to come by on an afternoon for a feast. While guests dine on his famous and fine duck prosciutto, bratwurst, coppa, and saucisson along with his homemade pickles, James cooks jambalaya in a gigantic pot out in the middle of his backyard. With little measuring and low-tech tools, he cooks up enough to offer seconds and take-home plates. He worked out this generous home-kitchen version, plenty for a good-size crowd, and it comes out wonderfully, whether you want a one-dish meal or a fantastic Louisiana-style star on a glorious and hearty buffet. James grew up in Louisiana's Cajun country, and his jambalaya features chile heat, but leaves out the chopped tomatoes essential for the Creole version. Jambalaya's roots lead back to the Spanish presence in Louisiana: Like the classic Spanish paella, this rice-and-sausage, seafood-laced one-pot dish is cooked outdoors over an open fire. For this recipe, you will need a large, heavy-duty pot with a tight-fitting lid, preferably cast iron or enameled cast iron. Next day it's even better, and freezing works if you have more than you can enjoy right away.

- 3½ pounds whole chicken or bone-in chicken pieces
- 1 tablespoon sweet or hot paprika or smoked paprika
- 1½ teaspoons salt
- 1 teaspoon freshly ground pepper
- 1 teaspoon cayenne pepper
- 1 teaspoon dry mustard
- 5 bay leaves
- 3 tablespoons lard, bacon fat, or vegetable oil
- 1½ pounds boneless pork, preferably pork butt or pork shoulder, cut into 1-inch chunks
- 1 pound smoked sausage, such as andouille or kielbasa, halved and cut crosswise into ½-inch chunks
- 2 cups chopped onions
- 1 cup chopped celery
- 1 cup chopped green bell peppers
- 2 tablespoons chopped garlic
- 2 tablespoons tomato paste
- 3 cups medium-grain or long-grain rice
- 1 cup chopped green onions

1 Place the chicken in a 4-quart pot or Dutch oven and add enough water to cover it by 1 inch. Place the pot over high heat and let it come just to a rolling boil. Quickly turn the heat to medium-low and simmer until the chicken is tender and cooked to the bone, 45 minutes to 1 hour.

2 In a small bowl, combine the paprika, salt, pepper, cayenne, and mustard and stir them with a fork to mix. Add the bay leaves.

3 Transfer the chicken to a platter and let it cool enough to handle. Measure the remaining chicken broth and set aside 6 cups. Reserve any extra for another use, or add water if needed to make 6 cups. Pull the chicken meat from the carcass, discarding all the skin and bones. Tear or chop the chicken into big, bite-size pieces. You will need about 3½ cups. Cover and reserve any extra for another use. →

4 Place a heavy-bottomed 6-quart pan, such as cast iron or enameled cast iron, over high heat. Add the lard just as it starts to smoke. Carefully place about half the pork on the bottom of the pan. Leave room so that the pieces are not touching. Let the pork sear, leaving it undisturbed until the meat begins to brown. As soon as it is handsomely browned on the bottom, toss it well. Continue cooking until the other sides have browned nicely, and then scoop it out onto a plate, leaving behind as much of the grease as possible. Avoid crowding the meat, and cook any remaining pork in the same way.

5 Next, add the sausage and cook, tossing often, until it is fragrant and evenly browned, 2 to 3 minutes. Scoop out the sausage onto the platter of browned pork and set aside.

6 Immediately add the chopped onions, celery, bell peppers, and garlic. Cook, tossing and stirring them constantly, until the mixture is fragrant, shiny, and softened, about 2 minutes. Add half the spice mixture and toss well to mix it evenly into the vegetables, about 1 minute. When most of the moisture has evaporated, turn the heat to medium-high and add the tomato paste. Continue cooking and stirring almost continuously for 2 minutes more.

7 Add the rice to the pan and stir to mix it in. Add the remaining spice mixture, the reserved pork, sausage, and chicken, and the 6 cups chicken broth. Stir well, making sure to scrape the bottom of the pan to remove any remaining debris and mix it into the broth. (Taste the broth at this point to assure the salt and spice are to your liking.)

8 Bring the mixture to a rolling boil. Stir well and then lower the heat to maintain a lively, visible simmer. Cover with a tightly fitting lid. Simmer until the rice has absorbed all the liquid and is tender, well-seasoned, and moist, 30 to 35 minutes. Remove from the heat and leave covered for 10 to 15 minutes. Remove the cover, add the green onions, and stir to mix them in evenly. Serve the jambalaya hot or warm.

Serves 8

Ya-Ka-Mein, New Orleans Style

The great and magical city of New Orleans serves up a feast of music, art, and creativity along with some of the world's finest food. If you're there enjoying Jazz Fest or dancing in a second line behind a big brass band, keep an eye out for Miss Linda Green. You'll be hungry, and her ya-ka-mein stand on wheels has the cure. Wherever NOLA folks congregate, Ms. Green serves up big to-go cups of tender noodles in a bodacious beefy broth, topped with green onions and hard-boiled egg. Tabasco and ketchup are on the side, and the noodle dish's nickname, "Old Sober," suggests its curative powers for the overserved. Ya-ka-mein has been on New Orleans menus for so long that its roots are a mystery. What's known is that you'll find it at corner cafés, take-out shops, and lunch spots if Ms. Green's stand isn't handy. Clearly, it's in the Asian noodle soup tradition, but how did it get here? From Chinese restaurants, or with U.S. troops who encountered it while serving overseas? And what about the similarly mysterious "yock"—Tidewater Virginia's satisfying tangle of linguine-like noodles with pork or chicken, chopped onions, ketchup, soy sauce, and cayenne pepper? I'm still searching for clues, while enjoying ya-ka-mein, cup by cup and bowl by bowl.

3 tablespoons vegetable oil

3¾ pounds bone-in chuck roast or pot roast, or 3½ pounds boneless beef stew meat

1½ cups chopped onions

1 tablespoon chopped garlic

½ cup soy sauce

1 tablespoon sugar

1 teaspoon salt

One 16-ounce box spaghetti

2 cups chopped green onions

8 hard-boiled eggs, peeled and halved lengthwise

Tabasco sauce or Crystal hot sauce for serving

Ketchup for serving

1 In a Dutch oven or large heavy saucepan, heat the vegetable oil over medium-high heat until a few drops of water sizzle at once. Add the beef and cook it undisturbed until it is fragrant and nicely browned on one side, 1 to 2 minutes. Turn and brown the other side to a handsome brown color, another 1 to 2 minutes. Turn it to brown the sides as well, and develop color and flavor without burning the beef, 3 to 4 minutes in all. Transfer the meat to a large plate and set it aside.

2 Add the onions to the pot and cook, tossing them often, until they are fragrant, shiny, and softened, about 2 minutes. Add the garlic and toss it well until it sends up its aroma, about 1 minute.

3 Return the beef to the pot, and add enough water to cover the meat. Bring it to a rolling boil. Adjust the heat to maintain an active boil and cook, skimming off and discarding any foam that rises to the top, for about 10 minutes.

4 When the foam has subsided, add the soy sauce, sugar, and salt and stir them in. Lower the heat to maintain a gentle but visible boil. Cook, turning the meat occasionally, until the meat is very tender, about 2 hours. →

5 When the meat is tender and the soup is nicely flavored, transfer the beef to a platter or baking sheet to cool. Cover the soup and keep it warm.

6 Bring a large pot of salted water to a wild boil. Cook the spaghetti until tender but not overcooked, 10 to 12 minutes. Drain it well, rinse it in cold water, and drain again. Return it to the cooking pot, add about 1 cup warm water to the bottom, cover, and set the pot aside on the stove over low heat to keep warm.

7 When the beef is cool enough to handle, discard the bones and excess fat, and chop it into big bite-size pieces. Return it to the soup and bring it to a gentle boil to make it nice and hot.

8 Place 1 cup of the cooked spaghetti in large individual serving bowls or big cups. Add a generous portion of the beef, green onions, and two halves of hard-boiled egg. Ladle on lots of hot soup and serve at once, with Tabasco and ketchup on the side.

Serves 6

Ropa Vieja, Little Havana Style

Naming this dish *ropa vieja*, which means "old clothes" in Spanish, shows a mischievous sense of humor, since it denotes a deliciously inviting dish, the last one you'd want to throw away. Ropa vieja consists of beef simmered slowly to such tenderness that it pulls apart into raggedy saucey shreds. The joke works, making those who know it long to eat it often and share the recipe. Adored in varying incarnations throughout the Spanish-speaking world, it takes minimal effort and yields grand results. My friend Sandra Gutierrez shares the Guatemalan version (*hilachas*), which includes potatoes, tomatillos, and annatto, in her essential cookbook, *Latin American Street Food*. Variations include capers, green peas, oregano, and wine. In Miami's Little Havana, cafés cook it this way, and serve it with rice, plantains, and *pan frito*, crunchy rich Cuban bread, buttered and grilled to crisp perfection for dipping in the sauce. We love it in warm tortillas for tacos, or chopped and tossed with noodles. Old clothes? Why, yes! Give me those comfy, easy ones we love to wear when we're relaxing at home.

- 2 pounds flank steak or beef brisket
- 2½ cups chopped onions
- 2 tablespoons chopped garlic
- ¼ cup olive oil
- 1 cup thinly sliced green bell pepper
- 1½ cups crushed or finely chopped tomatoes, with juice
- ¾ cup finely chopped carrots
- ¾ cup finely chopped celery
- ¾ cup small green Spanish-style olives, stuffed with pimientos
- 1 teaspoon ground cumin
- 1 teaspoon salt
- 1 teaspoon freshly ground pepper

1 Combine the flank steak, 1 cup of the onions, and 1 tablespoon of the garlic in a large Dutch oven. Add enough water to cover the meat. Bring it to a lively boil over medium-high heat.

2 Cook for 5 minutes, skimming off and discarding any foam that rises to the top. Lower the heat to maintain a visible, active simmer, and cover the pot. Cook for 1½ to 2 hours, until the meat is very tender, such that you can easily shred it. Remove the pot from the heat and let the meat cool in the stock for 30 to 40 minutes. Transfer the beef to a large bowl to cool completely. Pour the stock into a medium bowl and set it aside.

3 Quarter the meat, cutting it lengthwise and crosswise to make four large pieces. Pull the meat into thin shreds using forks or your hands. Cover and set it aside.

4 In the same Dutch oven, heat the olive oil over medium-high heat until a bit of onion sizzles at once. Add the bell pepper and remaining onions and toss them well. Cook, tossing them often, until they are fragrant, shiny, and softened, 2 to 3 minutes. Add the remaining garlic and toss it. Add the tomatoes and 2 cups of the reserved beef stock.

5 Increase the heat to medium-high and bring everything to a lively boil. Add the carrots, celery, and shredded beef. Stir well and cook for 5 minutes, stirring often. Lower the heat to maintain an active simmer and cook, stirring and scraping often to prevent sticking and burning, until the meat is very tender and the sauce has thickened, 20 to 30 minutes. Add more beef stock or water if needed to keep the stew from sticking or becoming dry. There should be lots of rich red sauce.

6 Stir in the olives, cumin, salt, and pepper. Remove the stew from the heat and serve it hot or warm.

Serves 4 to 6

Grillades and Grits

Luscious long-simmered sauce and tender cutlets of beef, veal, or pork make for a beloved breakfast or brunch centerpiece dish in both Creole and Cajun traditions. Unlike most Louisiana stews, this one traditionally comes with grits rather than rice. Typically made from round steak cut into squares and pounded out to tenderize the meat, grillades are pan-fried in lard and then simmered in gravy flavored with onions, bell peppers, celery, and tomatoes. *The Picayune Creole Cookbook* waxes eloquent about it, and revered Louisiana chef John Folse traces this dish's origins to the annual *boucheries* in south Louisiana, where family and community gathered to butcher hogs and prepare the meat for the next year. Baked cheese grits are a popular modern accompaniment, but everyday grits work fine, as do rice, couscous, or mashed potatoes.

1½ pounds beef round steak (see Note), cut into 2-inch squares
2 to 3 teaspoons salt
1 to 2 teaspoons freshly ground pepper
About 1 cup all-purpose flour
¼ cup lard, bacon grease, or vegetable oil
1 cup chopped onion
¾ cup chopped celery
½ cup chopped green bell pepper
3 tablespoons chopped garlic
3 cups Chicken Stock (page 152)
1½ cups chopped tomatoes, with juice
⅓ cup chopped green onions
⅓ cup chopped fresh flat-leaf parsley
Everyday Grits (page 155) or Grits Casserole with Garlic and Cheese (page 157) for serving

1 Spread out the steak pieces on a baking sheet in a single layer. Mix the salt and pepper together in a small bowl, and pour the flour onto a plate or large shallow bowl. Season the meat by sprinkling salt and pepper on both sides, and then dip each piece in the flour. Shake off excess flour, place the meat back on the baking sheet, and continue preparing the remaining meat.

2 In a large, deep, heavy skillet or a Dutch oven, heat the lard over medium-high heat until a pinch of flour blooms at once when added to the lard. Add enough of the seasoned beef to fill the pan without crowding, and cook it on one side until nicely browned, 1 to 2 minutes. Turn it, brown the other sides, and transfer to the baking sheet while you brown the remaining meat.

3 When the meat is browned, quickly add the onion, celery, and bell pepper to the hot grease and cook, tossing often, until they are fragrant, shiny, and softened, about 2 minutes. Add the garlic and toss it well. Add the stock and tomatoes and stir gently to combine everything. Return the beef to the gravy, nestling it down in the sauce, and lower the heat to maintain a gentle simmer. Cook, stirring now and then and adding a splash or two of water if needed to keep the gravy from sticking, until the grillades are tender, 40 to 55 minutes. Stir in the green onions and parsley and serve hot or warm, with or over the grits.

NOTE: *Traditionally, the beef is seasoned and pounded out to make for tender, thin pieces of meat. You can skip this step if you prefer and just cook the squares of beef as they are, allowing a little extra cooking time and adding a little extra liquid if needed. Pounding makes for great tenderness, but either way these will be so good.*

Serves 4 to 6

Nassau Grits, Pensacola Style

You don't have to go all the way to the Bahamas to try this hearty grits-centric breakfast dish. Instead, get yourself to Pensacola, Florida, where this satisfying repast is known, loved, and served up for breakfast and lunch, back as far as anyone can remember. There, at the legendary breakfast and lunch spot known as The Coffee Cup, Nassau grits can accompany breakfasts of cheese omelets, pork chops, or enormous biscuits with tomato-rich Spanish sauce. In the Lowcountry of South Carolina and Georgia, grits break free of their breakfast-only designation and show up all day long. With these tomato-enhanced grits, you can see why, whether you're having fried fish, or a big old-school burger. While Nassau grits are generally considered a side, I love them as a main course, given their doubly porcine combo of bacon and ham. Make them meatless and you have a handsome, intensified take on grits, perfect for a brunch menu or as an accompaniment to salmon, seafood, or summer vegetables off the grill.

- 1 quart water
- 1 teaspoon salt
- 1 cup grits, preferably stone ground
- 4 bacon slices
- 1 cup chopped onion
- ½ cup chopped green bell pepper
- 1 tablespoon chopped garlic
- 1½ cups peeled, chopped tomatoes, fresh or canned
- ¼ cup chopped ham

1 Combine the water and salt in a medium saucepan and bring them to a rolling boil over medium-high heat. Slowly pour in the grits, stirring constantly with a fork or a large spoon. Mix energetically, stirring and scraping to dissolve the grits into the water without lumps. Let the mixture come back to a lively boil, and stir well. Lower the heat to maintain a lively simmer and cook, stirring often, until the grits are thickened, softened, and a pleasing texture, 15 to 20 minutes for standard grits and 30 to 40 minutes for stone-ground, whole-grain grits. Remove them from the heat and set aside.

2 In a heavy medium skillet, fry the bacon over medium-high heat, turning as it begins to brown, until it is curled up and crisp. Remove the bacon and set it aside, leaving the grease in the skillet.

3 Quickly add the onion, bell pepper, and garlic to the grease. Cook, tossing them often, until the vegetables are shiny, fragrant, and softened, about 3 minutes.

4 Add the tomatoes and stir to mix them in. Bring them to a gentle boil and then lower the heat to maintain a gentle simmer. Cook, stirring now and then, until all the ingredients have combined into a flavorful thick sauce, 15 to 20 minutes. Check the grits often to stir them back into an evenly textured mixture, scraping the pot well. Meanwhile, chop the cooled bacon into small pieces and set aside.

5 Add the chopped ham and bacon to the tomato mixture and cook for 5 minutes more. Scrape the tomato–bell pepper mixture into the saucepan full of grits. Stir and scrape the pot to combine them evenly. Transfer the mixture to a serving bowl and serve it hot or warm.

Serves 4 to 6

Sallie Ann Robinson's Neck Bones, 'Tada, and Tomato Soup

Sallie Ann Robinson was born and raised in the Gullah community of Daufuskie Island, a world of profound natural beauty and cultural strength. One of the Sea Islands off the coastline of South Carolina and Georgia, Daufuskie is just a boat ride away from the city of Savannah. The title of her cookbook-memoir expresses the abundance, wit, color, and complexity of her world: *Gullah Home Cooking the Daufuskie Way: Smokin' Joe Butter Beans, Ol' Fuskie Fried Crab Rice, Sticky-Bush Blackberry Dumpling, & Other Sea Island Favorites*. Gullah cooks make the most of what can be raised, caught, gathered, or bought for the table. Pork neck bones, also known as pork collar, provide sweet, flavorful, and tender meat. Stewing solves the problem of getting it off the bones. Cooked gently with onions, tomatoes, potatoes ('tadas), and smoked meat, the bones deliver richness and robust flavor, especially after the soup gets a chance to rest and develop its flavor. Thick, meaty country-style pork ribs substitute nicely for neck bones, as do pork shoulder or pork butt. For smoked neck bones, you can use smoked turkey wings or turkey legs, or a link or two of smoked pork sausage such as andouille or kielbasa, chopped into 1-inch chunks.

- 1 pound fresh pork neck bones, pork shoulder, pork butt, or boneless country-style pork ribs
- ½ pound smoked pork neck bones or smoked turkey wings or leg
- 3 cups stewed tomatoes
- 1½ cups chopped onions
- ¾ cup chopped green bell pepper
- ½ cup chopped celery
- 1½ pounds peeled white or red potatoes, chopped into large chunks
- 1 teaspoon salt
- 1 teaspoon freshly ground pepper

1 Blanch the fresh and smoked neck bones by placing them in a large stockpot with enough warm water to cover. Bring the pot to a rolling boil over high heat and boil for 15 minutes. Drain and rinse the neck bones and return them to the pot.

2 Add 6 cups warm water to the pot and bring it to a rolling boil over high heat. Add the tomatoes, onions, bell pepper, and celery and turn the heat to medium-high. Bring it to a rolling boil again, and then adjust the heat to maintain an active simmer. Cover and cook, stirring occasionally, until the meat is tender and easy to pull off the bones, 50 to 60 minutes. Using tongs, transfer the meaty bones to a platter and set aside to cool.

3 Stir the potatoes, salt, and pepper into the pot (not the meat) and continue cooking at a lively simmer until the potatoes are tender, 15 to 20 minutes. While the potatoes are cooking, take the meat off the bones and chop it coarsely. Discard the bones and return the chopped meat to the pot. Stir the soup well, until the meat is warmed through. Serve it hot or warm.

Serves 10 to 12

Hall Family Ham-Bone Soup

My cousin Libbie Hall grew up in Durham, North Carolina, at a table abundant with her father's favorite Tennessee-style dishes as well as the standard goodness of the Piedmont region in North Carolina. We share sweet memories of holidays, family reunions, and easy summers on our maternal grandparents' dairy farm near Hillsborough. She loves this soup, which her mother made at least twice a year, using ham bones from Christmas and Easter feasts. A trained chef who grew up on her mom's excellent home cooking, Libbie has boosted the flavor of this recipe with cumin, cayenne, chipotles, and her favorite barbecue sauce. She makes it in an enormous pot passed down to her husband, Bob, from his German grandmother. Bob likes it best on day three, after the flavors have deepened, while son Jace strains out the meat and vegetables to savor just the incredibly tasty broth. Libbie loves both the particular recipe and the tradition of making her mother's soup, in batches big enough to share with her sister Edna's family, who live nearby. Libbie says to use whatever vegetables you have on hand, and to make a big batch and freeze portions for future winter-night suppers, along with hot cornbread, biscuits, saltines, or a side of rice.

- 3 tablespoons vegetable oil
- 2 cups chopped onions
- 1½ cups finely chopped carrots
- 1 cup finely chopped celery
- ¼ cup finely chopped garlic
- 1 tablespoon ground cumin
- 2 teaspoons salt
- 1 teaspoon freshly ground pepper
- ½ teaspoon cayenne pepper
- 6 cups Chicken Stock (page 152) or water
- 1 quart tomato juice, preferably V8 Juice
- 2 large chipotle chiles canned in adobo sauce, finely chopped
- 1 meaty ham bone
- 2 cups peeled and chopped red or white potatoes
- 1½ cups chopped ham
- 1½ cups black-eyed peas, frozen or canned, rinsed and drained
- 1⅓ cups fresh, frozen, or canned corn
- 1 cup chopped yellow squash
- 1 cup chopped zucchini
- 2 tablespoons barbecue sauce

1 In a large stockpot or Dutch oven, heat the vegetable oil over medium heat until hot. Add the onions, carrots, celery, and garlic and toss them well. Cook, tossing them often, until the vegetables are fragrant, tender, and just beginning to brown, 5 to 7 minutes.

2 Add the cumin, salt, pepper, and cayenne. Toss to mix them in evenly.

3 Add the stock, tomato juice, chipotles, and ham bone. Cover the pot and bring it to a lively boil. Lower the heat to maintain an active, visible simmer and cook, stirring occasionally, for 1 hour.

4 Increase the heat to bring the soup back to an active boil, and then add the potatoes, ham, black-eyed peas, corn, squash, zucchini, and barbecue sauce. Stir well and continue cooking until all the vegetables are tender, about 20 minutes more. Remove from the heat and serve the soup hot or warm.

Dumplings: *Satisfying Substance in a Bowl*

NOTHING STRETCHES A POT OF SOUP or stew like handmade dumplings, and Southern cooks have ways of making this frugal move seem like a bonus rather than a sign of want. Here you'll find two versions of this thrifty genre, in which dumplings, made from wheat flour, might remind you more of noodles than of plump bouncing pillows popular around the country. Made from flour mixed with the soup broth, these flat, thin, chewy dumplings go by several names. In North Carolina's Piedmont, I grew up eating them in the definitive version of the dish known as chicken and dumplings. Research into foodways taught me that in eastern North Carolina, heading toward the coast, they are rolled out super-thin and known as "pastry," where the same dish goes by the name chicken and pastry. Down on the Outer Banks, these long strips of chewy goodness are known as "pie-bread," even though the dough isn't exactly what is rolled out into a crust for pies.

You'll also find a wonderful recipe for fluffy, bouncy, round, and delightful dumplings from the Blue Ridge Mountains. There are two takes on cornmeal dumplings, sturdy and pleasing little disks of cornmeal goodness that are shaped by hand and dropped into stew pots to poach on the top of the ingredients. Moving in another direction, this chapter offers up two quirky dumpling-like dishes: Alsatian-style beef brisket in red soup with Creole matzoh balls, and a plain, simple, and super-easy crowd pleaser known as "saltine cracker stew," the kind of dish that you can remember the first time you make it, which is good, because I think you will want to make it again. ●

Serves 4 to 6

Mildred Council's Country Bonnet Green Peas with Dumplings

This essential dish is family fare, with home cooks turning a cup of flour, an apronful of English peas, and a pot of water with butter and salt into a worthy and satisfying meal. If you have fresh English peas from the garden, use them here. If not, go for frozen. Most of the year, that is what I have, and they make a memorable soup. I've adapted this recipe from *Mama Dip's Kitchen* by Mildred Council, a treasury of classic Southern recipes from her lifetime of working as a private chef, caterer, and award-winning restaurateur. What a privilege it is to live where Mrs. Council's restaurant is just ten minutes from my home! You will need about 3 pounds of fresh peas in their pods to yield 3 cups of shelled peas.

3 cups shelled fresh green peas, or two 10-ounce packages frozen peas

¼ cup butter, cut into pieces

Salt

1 cup all-purpose flour

1 In a medium saucepan, stir together 1 quart water with the peas, butter, and 1 teaspoon salt. Bring them to a lively boil over medium-high heat. Lower the heat and simmer for about 15 minutes for fresh peas, and 8 to 10 minutes for frozen, until the peas are tender. Remove the pan from the heat and set aside.

2 In a medium bowl, combine the flour with ⅓ cup of the pea broth and stir well. You will have a raggedy bowlful of dough. Using your hands, press and push it into a lump and then knead it a few dozen times, until you have a fairly smooth, springy dough.

3 On a lightly floured work surface, roll the dough out into a big, thin round. Cut it into long slender strips, and then cut each strip into lengths about 1 inch wide and 2 inches long, or smaller.

4 Return the pan of peas to the heat and bring it to a rolling boil once again. Drop in the dough pieces, one by one, until all the dumplings have been added. Stir as you go to mix everything together. Add water if needed to keep a pleasing portion of soup broth in addition to the peas, and simmer about 10 minutes more. When the dumplings are tender and chewy like good pasta and the peas are sweet and tender, taste for salt and adjust if need be. Ladle into bowls and serve hot. ●

Serves 10 to 12

Southerners love greens, but choosing a favorite? That we cannot do. Collard, mustard, turnip? Creasie, dandelion, kale, spinach? We love them all and why would we not? Deeply colored, sturdy-textured, and packed with nutritious goodness, greens are humanity's friend. Unlike lettuce, most of the greens Southerners cherish benefit from heat and time. The tradition of boiling up a big potful of greens goes back centuries and across the Atlantic to West African cuisines. The cooking juices, what's known in the South as "pot likker," always counted, too. Given that greens grow easily in gardens and in the wild, and that a little salt pork transforms their cooking liquid into a marvelous and satisfying soup, stewed greens took root in the South. Cornmeal in its various forms goes perfectly with greens, as a scoop of Spoon Bread (page 160), a crumbly hunk of Skillet Cornbread (page 159) on the side, or as dumplings simmered right in the pot. Traditionally, greens are seasoned at the table, as Edna Lewis reminisces in her cookbook *In Pursuit of Flavor*: "When I was growing up in Virginia, every house had a round tray on the table holding bottles and jars of oil, vinegar, mustard, salt, pepper, and sugar so that everyone could season their own greens."

Collard Greens with Pot Likker and Dumplings

- 8 ounces bacon, preferably thick-cut, or side meat or streak o' lean
- 5½ cups roughly chopped collard greens or other sturdy greens
- 1¾ teaspoons salt
- 1 cup cornmeal, white or yellow, preferably stone ground
- 2 tablespoons all-purpose flour

1 In a stockpot or large Dutch oven, cook the bacon over medium-high heat until it becomes fragrant, curly, handsomely browned, and crisp. Add 3 quarts water to the pot and bring it to a rolling boil over high heat. Stir the water and then lower the heat to maintain a visible simmer. Cover the pot and simmer it for 1 hour.

2 Using a slotted spoon, transfer the bacon to a medium bowl and set it aside to cool. Increase the heat to high, and let the pot return to a rolling boil. Stir in the greens and 1 teaspoon of the salt. Let the pot come back to a rolling boil, and then turn the heat to low. Cook, uncovered, stirring occasionally, for 45 minutes. When the bacon has cooled, chop it into 1-inch pieces and return it to the pot.

3 In a medium bowl, stir together the cornmeal, flour, and remaining ¾ teaspoon salt. Add ½ cup water and stir to combine everything into a thick, sturdy dough.

4 Set out a plate to hold the dumplings as you shape them. Wet your hands well with water and scoop out a generous 1 tablespoon of the dough. Gently roll it into a small ball, and then flatten it a bit into a patty, in the neighborhood of 1½ inches in diameter and ½ inch thick. Set this dumpling on the plate and continue making all the dough into dumplings.

5 After the greens have cooked gently for 45 minutes, increase the heat to bring the pot likker to a lively boil. Carefully place the dumplings all around the edges of the pot, on top of and encircling the bubbling greens. Continue adding dumplings, working inward, until you have used up all the dough. Using a ladle or a large spoon, scoop up pot likker and spoon it over the dumplings to moisten them as they cook. Lower the heat to maintain a lively simmer, cover the pot, and cook until the dumplings are tender and cooked through to the center, about 20 minutes more.

6 Remove the pot from the heat and let it stand for 5 minutes. Serve the greens, dumplings, and pot likker hot or warm. You can serve the pot likker on the side, in heavy glasses or mugs, along with the greens and dumplings. ●

Serves 6 to 8

Nancy Lloyd Suitt's Old-School Chicken and Dumplings

I love this satisfying, substantial, and simple stew for its goodness and because I learned it from my maternal grandmother Nancy Lloyd Suitt. It's all about the chicken and the broth it creates in cooking. Since my grandmother raised chickens, and never ran out of flour, this was a frequent pantry-centered supper from her dairy farm kitchen, and I love that you'll still find it in cafeterias, meat-and-threes, and other homespun locations throughout the Southern states. Miss Nannie, as she was widely known, would not have dreamed of serving anything resembling raw lettuce with this, but I love it with a big crisp and cool salad on the side, or even a plate of sliced tomatoes and a bowl of refrigerator pickles made with cucumbers, onions, and fresh dill. Today's supermarket birds can be huge five-pounders and more. That's great for feeding a crowd, and you can just make more dumplings and use more water. However, should you be desirous of a smaller version, just use chicken pieces, as long as they are bone-in and skin-on to flavor your stock.

- 3½ pounds bone-in skin-on chicken pieces
- 2 cups all-purpose flour
- 1 teaspoon salt
- ½ teaspoon freshly ground pepper

1 Place the chicken in a large deep pan such as a Dutch oven or a saucepan. Add enough water to cover the chicken pieces by about 1 inch. Place the pot over medium-high heat and bring it to a gentle boil.

2 Lower the heat to maintain a lively simmer and cook for 35 to 45 minutes, or until the chicken is tender and cooked to the bone. Remove it from the heat. Using tongs, transfer the chicken pieces to a platter and let them cool to room temperature. Set the chicken stock aside as well.

3 When the chicken is cool enough to handle, remove and discard the skin and bones and pull the meat into big pieces. Cover and refrigerate it.

4 Meanwhile, combine the flour, salt, and pepper in a medium bowl, using a fork. Make a well in the center of the flour and pour in about ¼ cup of the hot chicken stock. Stir well with the fork, until the flour comes together into a rough, shaggy dough. Turn it out onto a floured cutting board or kitchen counter, and knead it for about 3 minutes, until you have a fairly smooth, resilient dough.

5 Scatter flour over a workspace. Divide the dough into three portions. Using a rolling pin, roll out each portion into a thin, flat sheet. Cut it into strips 1½ to 2 inches wide. Cut the strips crosswise into pieces about 2 inches long.

6 Measure the chicken stock; you should have about 7 cups. If you don't have that much, add water to make 7 cups. Bring the chicken stock to a lively boil. Add the dumplings, a few at a time, stirring to keep them from sticking together. When all the dumplings are in the pot, stir well.

7 Lower the heat to maintain a very gentle simmer, cover, and let the dumplings cook 20 minutes, until they have thickened a little and become silky smooth outside and cooked within. Return the chicken pieces to the pot. Cook and stir gently to combine everything and heat the chicken pieces through.

8 Serve the stew in shallow bowls, with dumplings, chicken, and broth in each bowl. ●

Serves 8

Sheri Castle's Watauga County Chicken Stew with Fluffy Dumplings

My friend Sheri Castle grew up near the town of Boone, in Watauga County, North Carolina, and though she has long lived down in the flatlands of the Piedmont, her "mountain DNA" adds deep flavor to her writing and recipes. I love her chicken and dumplings recipe, which is different from what my grandmother made. "There are as many ways to make chicken and dumplings across the South as there are ways to fry the bird," Sheri notes. "Local loyalties run deep, and people have their favorites. The style used in this recipe hails from my pocket of the Blue Ridge Mountains. We make fluffy biscuit-like dumplings and let them float like clouds atop a simple stew studded with chunks of chicken, bright-orange carrots, and flecks of herbs. This dish is so comforting that it feels restorative." It would be lovely for someone who is under the weather, but it's fantastic when you're well, too. This has some steps, but not one of them is difficult or finicky, and the results repay you for every moment and each effort. Such beautiful soup—bubbling up around the fluffy dumplings, perfuming your kitchen, evoking grins from everyone at your table.

CHICKEN STEW

- 3¾ pounds whole chicken
- 4 cups Chicken Stock (page 152)
- 3 cups very coarsely chopped whole onions, peel and all, plus 1 cup chopped
- 2 cups very coarsely chopped carrots, washed but not peeled, plus 1½ cups chopped
- 2 cups very coarsely chopped celery, including leaves, plus ¾ cup chopped
- 3 garlic cloves, crushed
- 6 fresh thyme sprigs, plus 2 teaspoons fresh thyme leaves
- 2 to 3 teaspoons salt
- 1 tablespoon butter or vegetable oil
- ½ teaspoon freshly ground pepper

DUMPLINGS

- 2 cups all-purpose flour
- 1 teaspoon salt
- 1 tablespoon baking powder
- ½ teaspoon sugar
- ¼ cup butter, cut into small cubes and chilled
- 2 tablespoons lard, vegetable shortening, or butter, chilled
- ¾ cup half-and-half, evaporated milk, or milk

- ½ cup chopped fresh flat-leaf parsley

1 To make the stew: Place the chicken in a large Dutch oven or stockpot and add the stock, coarsely chopped onions with peels, coarsely chopped carrots, coarsely chopped celery with leaves, garlic, thyme sprigs, 1 teaspoon of the salt, and enough water to cover the chicken. Bring it to an active boil over medium-high heat. As soon as it boils, lower the heat to maintain a gentle but visible simmer until the chicken is cooked to the bone, 45 minutes to 1 hour. Using tongs, transfer the chicken to a large platter or bowl, leaving the chicken broth and vegetables in the Dutch oven. Remove the skin and bones from the chicken and add them to the broth. Continue cooking the broth over medium heat for 45 minutes more. →

2 Meanwhile, shred or chop the chicken into big, bite-size pieces. Cover and refrigerate it. Strain the broth into a large bowl and discard the bones and vegetables. Measure the broth; you should have about 8 cups. If you don't have that much, add water to make 8 cups.

3 Heat the butter in a Dutch oven over medium heat. Add the chopped carrots, chopped onion, chopped celery, thyme leaves, and remaining 1 teaspoon salt; stir to coat. Cook, stirring often, until the vegetables begin to soften, about 8 minutes. Add the reserved broth and simmer until the vegetables are tender, about 10 minutes.

4 Season with the remaining 1 teaspoon salt, if needed, and the pepper. Stir in the reserved chicken and heat it through. Keep the stew warm over low heat.

5 To make the dumplings: Put the flour, salt, baking powder, and sugar in a medium bowl. Use a pastry blender or your fingertips to work in the butter and lard until the mixture is crumbly and flecked with thin flakes of fat. When pressed against the back of your thumb, a bit of the mixture should cling like a small leaf. Slowly stir in the half-and-half. The dough should be soft and sticky, but firm enough to hold together on a spoon.

6 Bring the chicken stew to a low boil over medium-high heat. Stir in most of the parsley, reserving a generous pinch to add at serving time.

7 Using a 1-ounce scoop or two spoons, make golf ball–size dumplings from the soft dough and place them gently on the surface of the stew, spacing them evenly around the pot.

8 Cover the pot and cook until the dumplings are firm, fluffy, and fairly dry on top, about 20 minutes. Sprinkle the reserved parsley over the dumplings and serve at once. ●

Serves 6 to 8

Raymond Andrews's Saltine Cracker Stew

When members of the Carrboro Civic Club get to talking about times gone by, the topic soon meanders around to food. All the senior members remember Mr. Andrews's saltine cracker stew. Back when Andrews-Riggsbee Tractor Company anchored the local merchant's corner at Greensboro and Main, Mr. Andrews occasionally cooked up a batch of this satisfying and delicious stew. Cold, rainy days inspired him, and though this was long before cell phones or text messaging, the word spread quickly. Many a Carrboro citizen just happened to drop by the store right around lunchtime, which was fine, as Mr. Andrews always prepared his specialty in quantity. What a gift that his daughter, Bobbie Andrews, put his recipe down on paper so that Carrboro could keep his traditional pot bubbling. To Mr. Andrews, the hot sauce wasn't optional, and his choice was always Texas Pete.

One 4-pound stewing hen
1 teaspoon salt
1 cup milk
¼ cup butter, cut into chunks
½ teaspoon freshly ground pepper
One 16-ounce box saltine crackers
2 or 3 dashes hot pepper sauce (optional)

1 Place the hen and salt in a stockpot, soup pot, or very large saucepan. Add enough water to cover the hen by about 1 inch. Place the pot over medium-high heat and bring it to an active boil. Adjust the heat to maintain a gentle but lively simmer and cook until the chicken is tender and cooked through, 45 minutes to 1 hour. (If you can easily pull the meat off the bone, the chicken is done.) Remove the pot from the heat and use tongs to transfer the chicken carefully to a large platter or a 9-by-13-inch baking pan, reserving the broth in the pot.

2 When the chicken is cool enough to handle, pull the meat from the bones and return it to the broth, discarding the skin and bones.

3 Bring the stew back to an active boil. Add the milk, butter, and pepper and stir well.

4 Crumble up the crackers with your hands and add them to the soup in batches. Stir often. When you've added all the crackers, sprinkle in the hot pepper sauce, if desired. Simmer until the crackers are soft and all the ingredients are evenly combined. Serve hot. ●

Serves 10 to 12

Carolyn Roberson's Gardner's Creek Rockfish Stew with Cornmeal Dumplings

My friend Carroll Leggett's writing captures the spirit and history of eastern North Carolina's people and places and, while food is not always the subject, it often figures in there by story's end. One of his meandering research expeditions took him to Roberson's Marina on Gardner's Creek, a tiny store in Martin County. It serves as a bait shop, canoe rental depot, boat ramp, map and directions resource, as well as a community center for locals and folks who come from far and near to experience the natural magnificence of the Roanoke River area. Its late proprietor, Carolyn Roberson, served up information, reservations, and advice on exploring the region's beauty, fishing for striped bass, or simply escaping the loud hectic everyday world for a few hours or days on the blackwater creeks and rivers of the Roanoke and Cashie Rivers. She made this stew with catfish and, during their spring spawning season, with the star catch of the river, rockfish or striped bass, which attract anglers from near and far.

STEW

- 1 pound bacon
- ½ pound fatback, side meat, salt pork, or streak o' lean
- 3 cups chopped onions
- 3 bunches green onions, chopped
- 1 tablespoon dried red pepper flakes
- 1 teaspoon salt
- 1 teaspoon freshly ground pepper
- 5 baking potatoes, peeled and sliced
- 3½ pounds rockfish or catfish fillets, chopped into big, bite-size chunks

CORNMEAL DUMPLINGS

- 1½ cups fine, white, non-self-rising cornmeal
- 1½ tablespoons all-purpose flour
- 1 teaspoon sugar
- ½ teaspoon salt

- 10 hard-boiled eggs, coarsely chopped

1 To make the stew: In a large, heavy skillet, fry the bacon, turning often, until it is fragrant, handsomely browned, and crisp to your liking. Transfer the bacon to a plate and all the bacon grease to a medium bowl, and set them aside to cool.

2 Remove and discard any skin present on the piece of fatback. Chop the fatback into 1-inch chunks. (If using another type of salty side meat, chop it into ½-inch chunks.) Scatter the meat in the skillet where you cooked the bacon and place it over medium-high heat. When the fatback begins to sizzle, adjust the heat to medium so that it fries the meat briskly but doesn't smoke or burn. Cook, turning as needed to allow the fatback chunks to brown and release oil into the pan. When the fatback is handsomely brown and crisp, transfer the meat to a plate and the fatback grease to the bowl with the bacon grease and set aside.

3 Place the chopped onions and all but 1 cup of the green onions in a large stockpot or Dutch oven. Add the bacon grease, fatback, and fatback grease to the pot, along with the red pepper flakes, salt, and pepper. Add enough water to cover the onions and meats by 2 inches. →

4 Bring the pot to a gentle boil over medium-high heat. Let the water boil for a minute or two, and then lower the heat to maintain a lively, visible simmer. Cook until the onions become so tender they fall apart, 25 to 30 minutes. Resist the urge to stir, as this is a layered stew start to finish.

5 When the onions are tender, add the potatoes, scattering them in on top of the onions without stirring. Let the water come back to an active boil, and then carefully add the rockfish, putting it on top of the potatoes. The soup broth should be visible, covering the potatoes and most of the fish. Add more water if needed, to cover the ingredients by an inch or two (and remember not to stir the pot).

6 To make the cornmeal dumplings: In a large bowl, combine the cornmeal, flour, sugar, and salt. Stir with a fork to mix everything together. Slowly add ½ cup warm water and stir with the fork to make a thick batter. Add more water as needed until you have a thick, moist batter that holds its shape well. Using your hands, shape the batter into small balls, each about the size of a walnut. Gently flatten them out a little, to about 1¼ inches in diameter.

7 Add the cornmeal dumplings, placing them on top of the rockfish. Lay them around the edges of the pot and then fill in the middle if you have extra.

8 Adjust the heat to maintain a gentle lively boil, and cover the pot. Cook until the rockfish is flaky and opaque throughout and the cornmeal dumplings are tender, about 30 minutes more. Shake the pot now and then, but don't stir, checking the water to be sure you have enough to avoid sticking and burning.

9 Remove the pot from the heat. Crumble the bacon and scatter it over the top of the stew. Scatter in the hard-boiled eggs and the reserved 1 cup green onions. Cover the stew and let it stand for 20 to 30 minutes before serving. Scoop out each portion from the bottom, cutting down through the layers, so that each serving includes every layer of stew. ●

Serves 8 to 10

Florence Weiland Schornstein's Red Soup with Brisket and Creole Matzoh Balls

Marcie Cohen Ferris's first book, *Matzoh Ball Gumbo: Culinary Tales of the Jewish South*, explores food's powerful role in connecting people and transmitting cultural traditions over time and place. Growing up in a Jewish family in Arkansas, Marcie's childhood table reflected both Jewish and Southern culinary traditions. She fondly recalls her mom's Rosh Hashanah dinners with roasted honey chicken, tzimmes, and noodle kugel, as well as suppers of matzoh ball soup, pole beans, and black-eyed peas cooked by her grandmother, Luba Tooter Cohen, in her Blytheville, Arkansas, kitchen. She grew up on rugelach and pound cake, Coca-Cola brisket and, thanks to the "... miracle of Crisco," Sabbath fried chicken. Cohen found Jewish cooks in New Orleans jazzing up their matzoh balls with Creole seasonings and adding them to the gumbo pot shortly before serving. A selection of recipes enhances the book, including this wonderful dish from the New Orleans kitchen of Florence Weiland Schornstein. A favorite choice as a first course for holiday meals, this hearty soup of brisket, tomatoes, and vegetables aplenty has roots in the French region of Alsace. The Creole matzoh balls enhance this wonderful classic soup.

RED SOUP WITH BRISKET

- 2 cups coarsely chopped green cabbage
- 2 cups 1-inch chunks peeled Yukon gold potatoes
- 1½ cups coarsely chopped onions
- 1½ cups 1-inch chunks peeled turnip
- 1 cup thinly sliced leeks or coarsely chopped green onions
- 1½ cups ½-inch slices carrots
- ½ cup chopped celery
- One 6-ounce can tomato paste
- 2 teaspoons kosher salt
- ½ teaspoon freshly ground pepper
- 2 pounds well-trimmed boneless beef brisket or chuck roast

CREOLE MATZOH BALLS

- 2 tablespoons vegetable oil
- ¼ cup finely chopped onion
- ¼ cup chopped fresh flat-leaf parsley
- 1 tablespoon Creole seasoning spice blend (see Note)
- 2 eggs
- 2½ ounces matzoh ball mix

- ½ cup chopped fresh flat-leaf parsley

1 To make the red soup with brisket: In a Dutch oven or soup pot, combine the cabbage, potatoes, onions, turnip, leeks, carrots, celery, tomato paste, salt, and pepper. Add 2 quarts water and stir to mix everything together. (There should be enough water to barely cover the vegetables. If not, add more, but do not make the soup too thin.) Add the brisket, and then bring the water to a rolling boil over high heat.

2 Adjust the heat to maintain a lively boil and cook for 10 minutes, skimming off and discarding any foam that rises to the surface. Lower the heat to maintain a very gentle simmer. Cook until the brisket is tender when pierced with a fork, 2½ to 3 hours. Remove the soup from the heat and transfer the brisket to a large platter to cool. Leave the soup covered. →

3 To make the Creole matzoh balls: In a small skillet over medium-high heat, warm 1 tablespoon of the vegetable oil until hot. Add the onion and cook, tossing often, until it is shiny and fragrant, about 2 minutes. Add the parsley and Creole seasoning and toss to mix everything. Remove from the heat and scoop the onion mixture into a medium bowl. Add the eggs and remaining 1 tablespoon oil and stir with a fork to blend the eggs and onion mixture together. Add the matzoh ball mix and stir to combine everything evenly. Cover and refrigerate for 20 minutes.

4 Meanwhile, chop the cooled brisket into 1-inch pieces and return them to the simmering soup. Stir well and keep covered.

5 Put 2½ quarts salted water in a large saucepan and bring it to a rolling boil over medium-high heat.

6 Wet your hands with cool water, shape the matzoh mixture into twelve balls, using a heaping 1 tablespoon mixture for each one. Drop the matzoh balls into the boiling water. Cover, turn the heat to low, and simmer until the matzoh balls are plump, fluffy, and cooked through, about 15 minutes. Using a slotted spoon, carefully transfer the matzoh balls to a platter.

7 To serve, bring the pot of soup to a lively boil over medium-high heat. Reduce the heat to maintain a lively simmer, and carefully add the matzoh balls. Gently stir in the parsley. Serve immediately.

NOTE: *Creole seasoning blends are available in the spice section of most supermarkets and also via mail order and online (see page 169). For this recipe, you can mix these ingredients together to substitute for the Creole seasoning blend: ½ teaspoon each of salt, black pepper, white pepper, cayenne pepper, paprika, and dried thyme, making a total of 1 tablespoon spices.* ●

7

Field Peas *and* Garden Beans, Fresh *and* Dried

LONG BEFORE EUROPEANS SAILED OVER and stepped onto Southern shores, the original Americans were tending beautiful, nourishing gardens, cultivating many varieties of beans and peas. Planted together with corn and squash, the other two of the "three sisters," their bean vines curled tendrils around growing cornstalks, winding their way up as the corn grew tall, and sending out beans and peas in delicious profusion. This agricultural bounty provided protein and satisfaction to the people, who knew how to prepare them in stews and soups, dumplings, small cakes, and fritters. To this day, green beans appear fresh on Southern summertime vegetable plates, often cooked with salt pork and new potatoes, and their presence on the pantry shelf after the annual summer canning marathon means vegetable pleasures throughout the winter. This chapter starts off with the "greatest hits" of the simple Southern bean repertoire, from fresh green beans, cooked low and slow with new potatoes and bacon, to field peas—including black-eyed peas, which are so beloved that they have two recipes all their own. Soup beans are here, a big pot of pintos with side meat and chopped onions on top; as are dried limas, so wonderfully textured and tenderly enrobed in their own amazing gravy. Red beans and rice are included, traditional on Mondays in New Orleans but too good to hold back and restrict to one day a week. From Cuban kitchens in Miami comes caldo gallego, an incredibly delicious stew with Spanish roots, hearty with sausage and greens. Rounding up this choir of good and pleasing dishes are an elegant but accessible version of Virginia's signature, peanut soup, and the classic from the Capitol kitchens, U.S. Senate Dining Room Bean Soup. On the menu there for more than a century, it's marvelous, deeply Southern, and certain to get your vote.

Serves 6 to 8

Green Beans with New Potatoes and Bacon

The thing about old-timey Southern-style green beans, cooked with some kind of salty pork and often studded with new potatoes, is that they are not overcooked. They are not crisp, crunchy, emerald green haricots verts that we forgot to take off the heat. Not everyone likes them, but then again, those of us who do like them, actually love them in all their tender, salt-infused, afternoon-green goodness, and we adore the pot likker they create as an extra gift. This is comfort food, a dear old family friend of a side-dish that I remember from family reunions, church homecomings, school cafeterias, and my grandparents' dinner table. You start with fresh green beans, tipped and tailed, strung if need be, and then snapped (as in snap beans) into 2- or 3-inch lengths before their low-and-slow cooking session. What do they go with? Pork chops? Fried chicken? Salmon cakes? Stew beef? Or a vegetable plate in summertime, with sliced ripe tomatoes, field peas, corn on the cob, cucumber salad, and a plate of cornbread squares, hoe cakes, or biscuits? Any and all of the above. I hope you like them, as I still do, even though I also dearly love the modern crisp-crunch of lightly cooked, shamrock-colored green beans.

- 4 bacon slices, cut into 1½-inch pieces
- 1½ pounds fresh green beans, trimmed and broken into 2- to 3-inch lengths
- ¾ pound new or russet potatoes, cut into 1- to 2-inch chunks
- ¾ cup chopped onion
- 1 teaspoon salt
- 1 teaspoon freshly ground pepper

1 Scatter the bacon over the bottom of a large saucepan or medium Dutch oven. Cook it over medium-high heat until sizzling, aromatic, and nicely browned on one side. Turn it over and cook it until curled up, browned, and fairly crisp.

2 Add the green beans, potatoes, and onion to the pan with the bacon. Add 3½ cups water, the salt, and pepper and bring the pan to a rolling boil over medium-high heat. Lower the heat to maintain an active, visible simmer, and cook until the beans are very tender and flavorful, and the potatoes are tender, 45 minutes to 1 hour. Serve the beans hot or warm.

Serves 4 to 6

Field Peas

Vigna unguiculata, anyone? Yes, please. When the subject is those pleasing little orbs known generally as field peas, what's in a name? These legumes have long been planted in fallow fields to nourish soil with nitrogen, earning them the name "field peas." Cows munch on them blissfully, hence the occasional name "cowpeas." Squared-off little ones fill their pods so tightly that we call them "crowder peas." Black-eyed peas, yellow-eyes, and purple hulls cue us with color, and October beans tell us when they'll be ready. Lady peas and cream peas are the only ones whose names stump me, but what really matters is getting them when they come in fresh and eating them, freezing them, or drying them for a year's worth of wonderful meals. They are, in fact, beans rather than peas, which you will know if you see them growing in pods or buy them unshelled. Southern cooks boost their impact with side meat: pork, salted and/or smoked and/or pickled, adding flavor, depth, protein, and pleasure. It's an economical use of one luxurious ingredient to season a cheap and satisfying side or main-event dish. At farmers' markets, you may find them shelled. Not cheap, but a bargain given the work of shelling a mess of peas.

- 1 pound shelled fresh or frozen field peas
- 1 cup chopped onion
- 1 tablespoon chopped garlic
- 2 teaspoons salt
- 1 teaspoon freshly ground pepper
- About 4 ounces chopped side meat, such as bacon, ham, or streak o' lean (optional)

1 In a 2-quart saucepan, combine the field peas, onion, garlic, salt, and pepper. Add enough water to cover the peas by a good inch. Add the side meat (if using).

2 Place the pot over medium-high heat and bring it to a lively boil. Skim off any foam that rises up and cook for 3 minutes. Lower the heat to maintain a lively, visible simmer and cook, stirring occasionally, until the peas are tender, 25 to 55 minutes, depending on what kind of peas and how old they are. Keep the water level replenished.

3 When the peas are tender, remove them from the heat, cover, and let them stand for 10 to 15 minutes. Serve them hot or warm.

Serves 6 to 8

Hoppin' John

According to Southern culinary tradition, setting yourself up for a new year filled with good fortune is easy: Just eat this beloved rice and peas dish known as hoppin' John on New Year's Day. Whether you stew the field peas and long-grain rice together in one pot, or combine cooked rice and field peas in the serving bowl, hoppin' John with a side of long-simmered greens will bring you good luck all year long. While black-eyed peas come to mind and to the table first and foremost, Lowcountry cooks are partial to red peas, a smaller, rust-colored cousin within the field pea family. Beloved throughout the Caribbean Islands, rice and pea dishes abound, made with red beans, black beans, lady peas, and pigeon peas, the latter known in Creole kitchens as *pois de pigeon*. Might the pronunciation of this particular pea be the seed of the nonsensical name "hoppin' John"? Could be. Fact is, we don't know, and probably never will. We know that hoppin' John makes for excellent eating, and is too good to save for one luck-seeking meal per year. Southerners love a jolt of flavor in this dish, provided by pepper vinegar, a tangy relish such as cabbage-based chow-chow, or some hot pepper sauce, along with an abundance of cornbread.

- ½ pound bacon, preferably thick-cut, or slices of side meat, streak o' lean, or salt pork (see Note)
- 2 cups dried black-eyed peas, soaked in cold water for 6 hours or overnight
- 1 cup chopped onion
- 1 teaspoon salt
- 1 teaspoon freshly ground pepper
- 1¾ cups long-grain rice

1 In a large pot over medium-high heat, fry the bacon until fragrant, crisp, and nicely browned. Remove the meat and set it aside to cool, leaving the cooking grease in the pot.

2 Drain the black-eyed peas and add them to the pot along with 6 cups water, the onion, salt, and pepper. Bring them to a rolling boil over medium-high heat. Stir well, and lower the heat to maintain a lively simmer. Cook uncovered, stirring now and then, for 1 to 2 hours, until the peas are very tender. Add a little water if needed to keep the water level visible in the pot.

3 Meanwhile, chop the fried bacon into 1-inch pieces and add it to the pot, stirring to mix it in well.

4 When the peas are tender, remove them from the heat. Drain the cooking liquid into a measuring cup to make sure you have 3 cups, adding more water if needed. Return the cooking water to the pot, pouring it back over the tender peas, and bring it up to a rolling boil. Quickly add the rice and stir it in.

5 Lower the heat to maintain a gentle but visible simmer and cover the pot. Cook undisturbed for 25 minutes, until the rice is tender. Remove the pot from the heat and let it stand, still covered, for 10 minutes. Remove the lid, stir gently, and serve hot or warm.

NOTE: *You could use a smoked ham hock in place of the bacon, cooking it in the actively simmering water for about 30 minutes before you add the black-eyed peas. Continue to cook it along with the peas and the rice. Remove it after cooking, cool, and chop any meat from the ham hock, and stir the meat into the pot before serving.*

Serves 6 to 8

Wilhelmina Toney Watkins's Black-Eyed Pea Stew

Food writer Heather Watkins Jones grew up nourished by the cooking and wisdom of her maternal grandmother, Wilhelmina Toney Watkins, known lovingly as "Mom-Mom." Born and raised in Hartsville, South Carolina, Mrs. Watkins moved to New Jersey as a young woman, packing her Southern cultural wisdom and culinary knowledge in her suitcase along with her tangible belongings. Heather loves cooking her Mom-Mom's stew on chilly days for its satisfying flavors, and also for its connections to her family's roots. She takes pleasure in sharing this family treasure with students in her cooking classes as well as with her daughters, hoping all of them will keep the love going by passing the recipe on.

- 3 tablespoons vegetable oil or lard
- 1½ cups chopped onions
- 1¼ pounds smoked ham hocks or hot Italian sausage
- 2 teaspoons chopped garlic
- One 14-ounce can crushed or diced tomatoes
- 1 quart Chicken Stock (page 152)
- 1 pound dried black-eyed peas
- ½ teaspoon salt
- ¼ teaspoon freshly ground pepper

1 In a large Dutch oven or stockpot, heat the vegetable oil over medium-high heat until a bit of onion sizzles at once. Add the onions and cook until they are fragrant, 3 to 4 minutes. Add the ham hocks and garlic, turn the heat to medium, and cook for 5 minutes more, stirring often so that the onions soften and wilt without much browning.

2 Add the tomatoes and cook, stirring often, for 5 minutes more. Add the stock, black-eyed peas, and 3 cups water. Increase the heat to bring everything to a boil, and stir well. Add the salt and pepper and adjust the heat to maintain a lively simmer.

3 Cover partially and cook, stirring now and then, until the peas are tender, about 2 hours. Remove the ham hocks and set them out on a plate until they are cool enough to handle. Remove the meat, chop it finely, and return it to the pot. Stir well. Serve the stew hot or warm.

Serves 8 to 10

Pableaux Johnson's Red Beans and Rice

My friend Pableaux Johnson believes we all need a signature dish, something satisfying and scale-able to crowd-pleasing quantities. His signature dish is red beans and rice, and he's been hosting friends for red-beans suppers for years. Usually he holds them in his light-filled second-story New Orleans kitchen, but he's been known to embark on a traveling red-beans adventure, for which he packs up pots and ingredients and takes his show on the road. Pableaux relies on classic Louisiana ingredients for this iconic dish: petite Caribbean-style Camellia-brand red beans, onions galore, andouille sausage from Jacob's in LaPlace, Tony Chachere's Creole seasoning (see Note), and Crystal hot sauce. He cooks his red beans on Monday nights, historically appropriate since this classic back-of-the-stove one-plate meal was traditionally The Dish for washday Mondays. On that day, cooks toiled all day long on laborious laundry, and the huge chore of hand washing for a big family left little time to focus on a complex meal. Pableaux knows the value of community, and his idea of making your own culinary tradition is as fine as his red beans. All you really need are a spirit like Pableaux's, a big pot, a stove, a table, and a hill of beans.

- 2 tablespoons vegetable oil
- 1½ pounds good smoked sausage, preferably andouille, sliced into coins
- 3 cups chopped onions
- 1½ teaspoons sweet or hot paprika
- 1½ teaspoons freshly ground black pepper
- 1½ teaspoons cayenne pepper
- 1½ teaspoons dried thyme
- 1 teaspoon salt
- 3 tablespoons finely chopped garlic
- 1 cup chopped celery
- 1 cup chopped green bell pepper
- 1½ pounds dried red beans, soaked in cold water for 6 hours, or overnight
- 1 tablespoon dried basil
- Pinch of rubbed sage
- 3 bay leaves
- 1 bunch green onions, chopped
- 1 bunch fresh flat-leaf parsley, chopped
- Hot sauce, such as Crystal
- Everyday Rice (page 154) for serving

1 Heat the vegetable oil in a large heavy pot. Add the sausage and cook, stirring often, until it is handsomely browned. Transfer it to a small bowl and set aside. Add the onions to the pot and toss them in the oil.

2 In a small bowl, combine the paprika, black pepper, cayenne, thyme, and salt and stir with a fork to mix them together. Add this seasoning mixture to the pot, and toss to mix everything together.

3 Cook over medium heat, stirring frequently, until the onions are fragrant, softened, and lightly browned, 3 to 4 minutes. Add the garlic and cook 5 minutes more, tossing often. Add the celery and bell pepper and cook, stirring often, until they are shiny, fragrant, and softened, 3 to 4 minutes.

4 Drain the red beans and add them to the pot. Cover them with fresh water. Rub the basil between the palms of your hands as you add it to the pot. Add the sage and bay leaves, along with the browned sausage. Stir well.

5 Bring the mixture to a lively boil, and then lower the heat and simmer, stirring occasionally, until the beans are tender, 1 to 1½ hours.

6 Scoop out about 1½ cups of the beans and liquid, placing them in a medium bowl and mashing them with a potato masher or a large spoon until the mixture looks creamy. Add them back to the pot and stir well.

7 Add the green onions and almost all of the parsley, reserving about ½ cup in a small bowl to be added at the table. Season the beans well with hot sauce. Serve the beans hot with the rice, reserved parsley, and more hot sauce.

NOTE: *Tony Chachere's Creole Seasoning could replace the paprika, black pepper, cayenne, thyme, and salt in this recipe. Use 2 tablespoons.*

Serves 4 to 6

Linda Rogers Weiss's Creamy White Limas with Ham and Caramelized Onions

My friend Linda Rogers Weiss grew up in Alabama and cherishes her culinary memories of fine, seasonal, regional Southern cooking, which nourished her from as far back as she can remember. A professionally trained chef, she knows the value of simple home dishes like dried limas cooked low and slow for a weekday dinner, which would nowadays be referred to as "lunch." I love what she told me about this recipe: "As long as I can remember, I have been eating these deliciously creamy lima beans. I think it's a part of some kind of initiation after you are born in the South, that you must learn to eat lima beans, with chopped onion on top, and a piece of cornbread on the side of the plate. My dad loved those big limas, too. I can remember how happy he was when he'd walk in the kitchen at dinnertime to find them on the table ready to be served." (Lunch in traditional Southern life could happen anywhere from noon to three, and was called "dinner," as opposed to "supper" in the evening.) Soaked and then simmered from morning through early afternoon, the lima beans turned creamy with a texture she compares to meat and gravy and just right for chilly days, with hot buttered cornbread on the side.

LIMAS

- 1 pound dried large lima beans
- 1 meaty ham bone or 8 ounces leftover ham, coarsely chopped
- 1 teaspoon salt

CARAMELIZED ONIONS

- 2 tablespoons olive oil or vegetable oil
- 2 tablespoons butter
- 3 cups thinly sliced sweet onions, such as Vidalia
- 1 teaspoon salt
- 1 teaspoon freshly ground pepper

1 To make the limas: Spread the lima beans out in a 9-by-13-inch pan and pick through them, discarding any withered ones or debris. Rinse the beans in a big strainer or bowl of water and drain well. Transfer the limas to a 3-quart pot or Dutch oven. Add the ham bone, salt, and water to cover them by 2 inches. Bring them to a rolling boil over medium-high heat.

2 Lower the heat to maintain a visible but gentle boil and cover the pot. Cook until the beans swell up plump, smooth, ivory-colored, and are meaty and very tender, 1½ to 2 hours. Check every 30 minutes, stirring and adding more water if needed to keep the water level just under the surface of the beans and prevent their drying out.

3 Meanwhile, make the caramelized onions: Add the olive oil and butter to a large skillet over medium-high heat. When the butter has melted and is foamy and bubbling, add the onions. Cook, stirring and tossing often, until the onions have become aromatic, softened, and handsomely golden brown, about 15 minutes. Add the salt and pepper and stir well. Set the onions aside until the limas are cooked.

4 Taste the lima beans for seasoning, transfer them to a serving bowl, and top with the caramelized onions. Serve them hot or warm.

Serves 4 to 6

Soup Beans with Chopped Onions and Cornbread

Throughout the South, people love pinto beans, cooked for hours to a state of creamy, pork-infused goodness, and served with chopped raw onions and hot cornbread on the side. The Mountain South loves them so profoundly that they've given them a name: Soup beans, usually pintos, but with navy beans and a few others included as well. Recipes seldom figure until you've come down to the flatlands and cities where I live. Dried beans, country ham or side meat, water, and a dried red pepper pod sums it up, but here is my measured-out version. I love spending time in the Blue Ridge Mountains of western North Carolina, where I remember ordering a traditional meal of soup beans with cornbread and chopped onions at a small cafe along the Parkway a few years back. I'd been away from the South for a decade at that point, and marveled at the plain, deep goodness and satisfaction provided in this old-time inexpensive meal. Shelled after harvest, pintos and other "shelly beans" like October beans, cranberry beans, and yellow eyes, dry as easily as they grow, and then keep beautifully. Shelled or not, soup beans see the people through, come what may, body and soul.

1 pound dried pinto beans, navy beans, or other shell beans, soaked in cold water for 6 hours, or overnight (see Note)

1 teaspoon salt

About 6 ounces side meat, such as salt pork, streak o' lean, bacon, or 1 smoked ham hock or meaty ham bone

1 cup chopped onion

Chow-chow or another relish or pickles, or tangy coleslaw for serving

Hot Skillet Cornbread (page 159) with butter for serving

1 Drain the beans. In a 4-quart saucepan or Dutch oven, combine the beans, enough water to cover them by 3 inches, and the salt. Bring them to a rolling boil over medium-high heat. Meanwhile, chop the side meat into three or four big chunks and add them to the pot. If using a ham hock, add it whole.

2 When the water is boiling, stir the beans and lower the heat to maintain a lively but gentle boil. Cook, stirring now and then, until the beans are very tender, 1½ to 3 hours. For creaminess, remove 1 cup of beans at the end of the cooking time, mash them well with a potato masher or a spoon, and return them to the pot, stirring them in.

3 Remove the pot from the heat and ladle out the beans hot or warm, in small soup bowls with lots of their cooking broth. Serve with the chopped onion, chow-chow, and cornbread with butter.

NOTE: *You can prepare the beans without the long soaking time by bringing them to a rolling boil in enough cold water to cover by 3 inches, boiling for 3 minutes, and then setting them aside for 1 hour. Drain them well and proceed as directed.*

Serves 8 to 10

Caldo Gallego, South Florida Style

This hearty bean-based soup, originally from the northwestern Spanish province of Galicia, has vibrant Cuban cultural influences today. Versions vary in terms of the particular ingredients you choose for the dish. The legumes could be navy beans, white beans, great Northern, or even garbanzo beans. The meat could be smoked ham, ham hock, or bacon, along with spicy chorizo or smoked pork links. Greens options include kale, collard, turnip, and spinach. Potatoes are required, while tomatoes are occasional, and saffron is a rare flourish. Given that northern Galicia borders Portugal, the resemblance of this fine soup to Portugese *caldo verde*, made with kale, linguiça sausage, and potatoes will come as no surprise. Whichever variation you choose, you will end up with a fine and satisfying pot of *caldo gallego*. Be sure to serve this with either rice or hot buttered bread for dipping in the robust soup.

- 5 bacon slices
- 1½ cups chopped onions
- 1 pound dried navy beans, soaked in cold water for 6 hours, or overnight (see Note)
- 6 ounces chorizo sausage (see Note), andouille, or smoked kielbasa
- 1 tablespoon vegetable oil
- 1 tablespoon chopped garlic
- 3 cups 1-inch chunks peeled potatoes
- 4 cups chopped turnip greens, mustard greens, collard greens, or Swiss chard
- 1 teaspoon salt
- ½ teaspoon freshly ground pepper

1 In a large Dutch oven, cook the bacon over medium-high heat until it sizzles, stirring as it begins to curl and brown, about 1 minute. Add the onions and cook, tossing them often, until both ingredients are shiny and fragrant, and the bacon is nicely browned, 3 to 4 minutes.

2 Drain the beans, add them to the pot, and stir well. Add enough water to cover the beans by 1 inch. Bring it to an active boil and stir the beans. Lower the heat to maintain a gentle, but visible, lively simmer, and cook for 1½ to 2 hours, until the beans are tender.

3 While the beans cook, cut the sausage lengthwise in half, and then crosswise into ½-inch chunks. Heat the vegetable oil in a medium skillet over medium-high heat until a drop of water sizzles at once. Add the sausage and cook, tossing it often, until it is shiny, fragrant, and nicely browned, 2 to 3 minutes. Add the garlic, toss it well, and set the pan aside.

4 When the beans are tender, stir the potatoes and turnip greens into the pot. Cook until the greens and potatoes are tender, 15 to 20 minutes. Add the sausage along with the garlic and the oil in which they cooked. Add the salt and pepper, stir well, and remove the pot from the heat. Serve the caldo hot or warm.

NOTE: *For a speedier version, instead of soaking the beans overnight, you could bring the dried navy beans to a rolling boil in enough water to cover them. Boil for 3 minutes, and then let them stand for 1 hour. Proceed with the recipe as directed. You also could use 5 cups canned navy beans, rinsed and drained.*

Look for fresh chorizo in the refrigerator case, resembling kielbasa or andouille sausage. I love this recipe with these fresh sausages, but you could also use Spanish-style chorizo, the dark red, harder-textured dried version, as well.

Serves 8

U. S. Senate Dining Room Bean Soup

This satisfying dish marries navy beans with ham hocks and onion and nothing but time, which is all it needs to coax deep goodness out of simple ingredients. Served in the dining rooms and cafeterias of the U.S. Capitol since the turn of the twentieth century, this substantial dish consistently wins votes across party lines, in a place where agreements can be difficult to reach. The Senate's version never varies, but you and I can use it as a canvas. Jazz it up with spicy condiments, proteins, seasoning pastes—whatever strikes your fancy. Curry paste or powder? Sausage or ham, crispy garlic or pesto? Play with it! It's a main course soup that costs little and keeps well. Plan ahead, as the ideal way to make this dish is to soak the beans overnight. I love this generous portion, wherein I cook once and freeze half of it for a future busy-day meal.

- 2 pounds dried navy beans or marrow beans, soaked in cold water for 6 hours, or overnight (see Note)
- 2 smoked ham hocks or 8 ounces cooked thick bacon or chopped ham
- 2 tablespoons butter
- 1½ cups chopped onions
- Salt
- Freshly ground pepper

1 Drain the beans well and place them in a large stockpot or Dutch oven. Cover them with hot water by 3 inches. Add the ham hocks and bring them to a gentle boil over medium-high heat. Lower the heat to maintain a lively, visible simmer and cook, stirring now and then, for 2 to 3 hours.

2 Begin checking the beans for tenderness after 2 hours. When they are very tender, remove the ham hocks and set them out on a platter to cool, leaving the beans to simmer gently a little longer. When the ham hocks are cool enough to handle, chop and pull away as much of their smoky meat as you can manage to get. (It won't be a huge amount: They've done their main job of flavoring the soup, and this is a small bonus.) Finely chop the meat and return it to the soup, discarding the bones, skin, and any inedible bits.

3 Heat the butter in a large heavy skillet until it is foamy and bubbling. Add the onions and cook, tossing them often, until they are fragrant, softened, and just lightly browned, 5 to 7 minutes. Add them to the soup, stir well, and cook for 5 minutes more. Add 1 teaspoon salt and 1 teaspoon pepper and check the seasoning; add a little more if needed. Serve the soup hot or warm.

NOTE: *If you need this soup now and can't wait for an overnight soaking of the beans, use the quick-soak method. Place the beans in a large saucepan with enough cold water to cover them by 3 inches. Bring them to a rolling boil over high heat. Cook for 3 minutes and then remove them from the heat. Let stand for 1 hour; then drain well, and proceed as directed.*

Serves 4 to 6

Hotel Roanoke Peanut Soup

Since 1882, the Hotel Roanoke in Virginia has welcomed travelers and diners to its massive, Tudor-style environs, first as a stopover on the Norfolk and Western Railway, and later as an elegant destination for tourists and business travelers en route to the Blue Ridge Mountains. The hotel's version of this Virginia classic, a beloved fixture on the menu since the 1940s, is simple to make and luscious to eat. Paired with the hotel's signature version of spoon bread, this creamy soup appears on the Thanksgiving buffet each year. Peanut soup's presence on Virginia tables shows the state's West African culinary heritage, with its tradition of satisfying peanut or "groundnut" stews such as *maafe* from Senegal and the Gambia. Here's my version of the celebrated soup, which we enjoy from early autumn to late spring.

- 2 tablespoons butter, olive oil, or canola oil
- ½ cup finely chopped onion
- ½ cup finely chopped celery
- 1 tablespoon all-purpose flour
- 1 quart Chicken Stock (page 152)
- 1 cup creamy or chunky peanut butter, ideally freshly ground
- ½ teaspoon salt
- 2 teaspoons fresh lemon juice or apple cider vinegar
- ¼ cup finely chopped roasted and salted peanuts (optional)

1 In a medium saucepan over medium-high heat, melt the butter. When it is bubbly and sizzling, stir in the onion and celery. Cook, stirring often, until the onion is fragrant, shiny, and softened, but not browned, 3 to 4 minutes. Add the flour and stir to mix it into the butter.

2 Add the stock and cook, stirring often, for 25 minutes. Stir in the peanut butter and salt and continue cooking, stirring often, until everything combines into a smooth, creamy soup, 1 to 2 minutes more. Add the lemon juice and remove the soup from the heat.

3 Transfer the soup to a serving bowl and serve it hot or warm, with chopped peanuts sprinkled over the soup, if desired.

8 Vegetables in the Stewpot, *All Year Long*

SOUTHERNERS LOVE THEIR GARDENS, and many folks while away winter evenings dreaming over their seed catalogs, making plans for visual beauty and edible plenty once the sun takes over for another growing season. Nowadays, that catalog might be an online resource rather than a paper booklet in the mail, or a combination of the two. *The Old Farmer's Almanac* continues to guide gardeners as well as farmers, and the ever-burgeoning community of farmers' markets around the South provides a jump-start for people like me, who love the idea of gardening but treasure the expertise and starter plants that need only a place in the dirt to start giving back.

My friend Sheri Castle's brilliant creation, *The New Southern Garden Cookbook,* provides an alphabetical introduction to every vegetable and fruit you could think of to plant or look for in the marketplace. If you love the recipes in this chapter, you will be delighted with the abundance of details, advice, and recipes she offers on everything from tomatoes and potatoes to rutabagas, asparagus, and peas. Her tomato gravy is included here, as are a bushel basket of recipes for mostly simple, supremely delicious, good-for-us vegetable-centered soups and stews.

These really are more soups than stews, the kind of dishes that make a sandwich into supper, or go along with sliced tomatoes, deviled eggs, and refrigerator pickles on an almost-too-hot-to-cook summer evening. Many of them are year-round dishes, especially the Blue Ridge Mountain Wild Mushroom Bisque (page 146), Grandma Harris's Fantastic Turnip, Mustard, and Collard Greens (page 147), and the luscious and refreshing Cool and Creamy Avocado Soup, Palm Beach Style (page 138). Even Sheri Castle's Tomato Gravy (page 149) is a wintertime favorite, because she told me it made a wonderful dish even with canned tomatoes, and it most certainly did. Whether you plant a garden and need ways to dispatch all those zucchini, or you come home from the supermarket determined to get some produce on the table more often, this chapter is a good little resource, a place to find everyday soups that you will enjoy eating and want to make again.

When summer saunters in and whispers in your ear that it might just be just too hot to cook, this green soup will serve you well. Quick as a sudden summer rainstorm and simple as cannonballing into the swimming pool, this dish comes together swiftly and then waits patiently for hours, chilling out and gaining flavor notes, regardless of how hard the afternoon sun is beating down. If you don't have buttermilk handy, you could replace it with milk and add a generous scoop of sour cream or yogurt to keep the tangy complexity in the mix. Fresh dill shines in this soup, but you could use just the parsley, green onions, or no herbs at all and still have a tasty cool soup. You will need a food processor, blender, or immersion blender for this recipe. Work in batches if you need more capacity than your machine allows.

Serves 4 to 6

Cool Cucumber Soup with Buttermilk and Fresh Dill

- 2 pounds cucumbers, such as Kirby, hothouse, or pickling, trimmed and peeled
- 1½ cups buttermilk
- 1 cup milk
- 1 tablespoon chopped fresh flat-leaf parsley
- 1 tablespoon chopped fresh dill
- 1 teaspoon salt
- 1 teaspoon freshly ground pepper
- 1 teaspoon sugar

1 Halve each cucumber lengthwise. Hold a cucumber half in one hand and hold a spoon upside down in your other hand, inserting its tip into the cucumber at the top where the seeds begin. Pull down, scooping out the seeds and leaving a cucumber canoe. Repeat with all the cucumbers and then chop them coarsely. You will need about 3¼ cups of cucumber chunks.

2 Place the cucumber chunks in a large bowl and add the buttermilk, milk, parsley, dill, salt, pepper, and sugar. Stir to dissolve the seasonings and mix everything together. Transfer the mixture to the work bowl of a food processor or the jar of a blender. Work in batches if need be. Process, pulsing on and off and stopping to scrape down the sides, until you have a beautiful, soft green soup, pleasingly textured and evenly combined. Serve it right away, or cover and refrigerate it until serving time, up to 1 day. Serve the soup cool or cold.

NOTE: *You could make this cool, refreshing soup by hand. Use a very sharp knife to chop the peeled, seeded cucumber halves very finely. Place them in a large bowl, add the remaining ingredients, and stir with a large spoon to mix everything evenly. Or combine the very finely chopped cucumber with all the remaining ingredients in a large jar with a tight-fitting lid and shake it up until everything is evenly combined.*

Serves 4 to 6

Cool and Creamy Avocado Soup, Palm Beach Style

This luxurious green soup invites you to lunch on the verandah in a lush seaside corner of Florida. It is inspired by a recipe in *The Florida Cookbook: From Gulf Coast Gumbo to Key Lime Pie*, by veteran journalists Jeanne Voltz and Caroline Stuart, which invites cooks and armchair travelers to sample Florida's extraordinary flavors, plain and fancy, coastal and inland. This elegant starter pleased guests in resort hotels from the 1880s through the 1920s. Make this satisfying soup in summertime, when you hunger for something substantial but simple to prepare. You can use a food processor or blender to purée the soup, or go old-school with a potato masher, pressing the soup through a strainer or sieve if you want it ultra-smooth. No cooking here, so if you're looking for a no-stove refreshing and gorgeous soup, this is your dish.

- 1½ cups avocado chunks (see Note)
- 2½ cups Chicken Stock (page 152), cold
- ⅓ cup fresh lime juice or lemon juice
- ¼ cup chopped green onions
- ½ teaspoon salt
- ¼ teaspoon freshly ground pepper

1 In a blender or food processor, combine the avocado with 2 cups of the stock, the lime juice, and green onions. Blend or process everything until very smooth, stopping to scrape down the sides.

2 Transfer the soup to a large pitcher or serving bowl. Add the remaining ½ cup chicken stock, along with the salt and pepper. Stir well. Serve the soup at once, or transfer it to a glass jar or other sealable container and refrigerate it for up to 2 days.

NOTE: *Cut about 1½ pounds ripe avocados in half lengthwise. Twist them apart, and remove and discard the large round seed. Using a large spoon, scoop out the flesh. Pack it loosely into a measuring cup to make a generous 1½ cups.*

Serves 4 to 6

Jenny Fitch's Creamy Spring Greens Soup

Gorgeously green and blooming with flavor, this wonderful soup can be on your table quickly. It is one of a big bouquet of flavorful and lovely dishes created by the late Jenny Fitch for *The Fearrington House Cookbook: A Celebration of Food, Flowers, and Herbs*. Worthy of company but not out of reach for a weeknight supper, it's the kind of cooking she loved—an elegant, satisfying soup from easy-to-gather ingredients, leaving her time to tend her roses and design beautiful spaces, indoors and out. She and her husband, R. B. Fitch, created the Fearrington House Inn, an AAA Five Diamond Relais & Châteaux property, from a landmark North Carolina dairy farm back in 1980. In springtime, she made this soup with spinach or creasie greens, a type of wild cress. Turnip greens work nicely in autumn, along with spinach and romaine lettuce. She served it hot, but I know from experience it makes a wonderful lunch, cold from the refrigerator, the day after it's made.

2 tablespoons butter
1½ cups chopped onions
6 cups Chicken Stock (page 152)
1¼ pounds red or white potatoes, peeled and chopped
1½ teaspoons salt
½ teaspoon freshly ground pepper
2 cups coarsely chopped creasie greens, watercress, or turnip greens (see Note)
1 cup coarsely chopped romaine lettuce
1 cup coarsely chopped spinach
1 cup heavy cream, half-and-half, or evaporated milk

1 In a large saucepan or small Dutch oven, melt the butter over medium heat until it bubbles. Add the onions and cook, tossing them often, until they are fragrant, shiny, and softened, but not browned, about 5 minutes.

2 Add the stock, potatoes, salt, and pepper and bring them to a boil. Lower the heat to maintain a lively simmer and cook, stirring occasionally, until the potatoes are tender, 15 to 20 minutes.

3 Add the greens, lettuce, and spinach and increase the heat to bring the soup back to a lively boil. Cook, stirring often, until the greens are tender but still brightly colored, 5 to 7 minutes more.

4 Remove the soup from the heat. Transfer it to a large food processor in two or three batches, and process to make a fairly smooth purée. Return the soup to the cooking pot and stir in the heavy cream. Serve the soup hot or warm; or cool it to room temperature, cover, and chill it for at least 2 hours.

NOTE: *If you've purchased your greens fresh from the fields, give them a thorough rinse before chopping. Fill a large bowl with cool water and plunge the greens in. Swish them around to loosen any dirt, and repeat if needed until the water stays clear. Drain well and then gather the greens up into stacks and chop them coarsely.*

Serves 4

Summer Squash Soup with Black Pepper and Thyme

Even a modestly successful gardener like me can find vegetable glory deep among the huge prickly leaves of summer squash. Until I was voting age, "squash" meant the curvy-necked yellow ones. We had no need to specify their color, any more than one would say "green cucumbers," since that's all there was to grow and eat. Then zucchini showed up in the supermarkets, making the summer vegetable plate an even more colorful and tasty option. I embrace both now, along with pattypan and any other squash-family member you place before me. Since summer squash are so tender, we need to eat them up while the sun beats down upon us all, and here is a quick and tasty way to do just that. If you prepare this soup ahead and chill it, taste for salt after you've reheated it, as chilling tends to mute the saltiness of soup.

- 2 tablespoons butter, olive oil, or canola oil
- ½ cup chopped onion
- 2 teaspoons chopped garlic
- Heaping 1 tablespoon chopped fresh thyme leaves, or 1 teaspoon dried thyme
- 3 cups chopped summer squash, yellow squash, or zucchini
- 2 cups Chicken Stock (page 152) or water
- 1½ cups milk
- Salt
- Freshly ground pepper

1 In a medium saucepan or small stockpot, melt the butter over medium-high heat until it sizzles and bubbles up, but doesn't yet brown. Add the onion, toss it well, and cook, stirring often, until it is fragrant and shiny, about 3 minutes.

2 Add the garlic and about half the fresh thyme, or all the dried thyme. Toss well, and add the summer squash. Continue cooking, tossing often, until the squash chunks are softened, shiny, and brightened in color, about 3 minutes more.

3 Add the stock and milk and stir them in. Bring them to a lively boil, and then adjust the heat to maintain a lively simmer. Cook for 10 minutes, stirring once or twice. If using fresh thyme, add the remaining thyme now. Remove the soup from the heat.

4 Transfer about one-third of the soup to a blender or a food processor, taking care since it is very hot. Blend or process it as smoothly as possible. Continue with the remainder of the soup in two more batches. Add ½ teaspoon salt and ½ teaspoon pepper, then taste the soup and add more, if you need it. Serve the soup hot or warm.

Serves 4 to 6

Ruby Lanier's Fresh Corn Soup

Summertime is fresh corn season all over the South, and enjoying it in soup extends possibilities for pleasures of the corny kind. This recipe comes from Mrs. Ruby Lanier, mother of my friend Carroll Leggett. Carroll is a brilliant writer and essayist who grew up in eastern North Carolina on fine, old-school home cooking and loves to share what he knows. His mother cooked simple bright-flavored soups even in summertime, fresh from her vegetable garden. In wintertime, Carroll makes this as a quick, busy-night supper, and serves it with his famous biscuits studded with hoop cheese, the kind of ultra-sharp Cheddar once sold in hunks wrapped in butcher paper at the dry-goods store. I love this bright, simple soup accompanied by a plate of thick-sliced Big Boy tomatoes, a bowl of cucumber salad, zucchini sautéed with garlic, and some Green Beans with New Potatoes and Bacon (page 120). Mrs. Lanier used only the white part of the green onion, but I include tops for their flourish of gorgeous greenness.

- 1½ cups fresh corn cut from the cob (see Note, page 148) or frozen white or yellow corn
- 1 cup finely diced red or white potatoes
- ½ cup thinly sliced green onions
- 3 tablespoons fresh thyme, or 2 teaspoons dried thyme
- 5 cups Chicken Stock (page 152)

In a large saucepan, combine the corn, potatoes, green onions, and thyme. Add the stock and stir to mix everything together. Bring it to a boil over medium-high heat, then lower the heat to maintain a gentle boil. Cover and simmer for 30 minutes, until the potatoes are tender. Serve hot or warm.

Serves 4

Lowcountry Okra and Tomato Soup

In the history of Southern cooking, this dish goes way, way back. Its essential ingredients, okra and tomatoes, comprise the original combination of crops connecting West Africa and America. This dish simmered away in cast-iron pots over open fires as well as in hearth kitchens indoors, from Williamsburg and Charleston through the Piedmont regions of North Carolina, Georgia, and beyond. Known and beloved in the Lowcountry as "okra soup," it also goes by "okra gumbo" and "stewed okra." It can be drier or juicier, depending on the proportion of tomatoes, cooked for hours over low and slow coals. Bacon or fatback is its standard start, but olive oil and garlic make a lovely version. Start with vine-ripe juicy tomatoes and petite pods of okra in the summertime, but know that a winter version made with canned tomatoes and frozen chopped okra brings wonderful flavor to your cold-weather menu. Cornmeal-based bread is not an official requirement here, but I find the pairing so pleasing that it's simply a matter of which kind: Corn Cakes (page 158) or Skillet Cornbread (page 159)?

- 2 tablespoons bacon grease, lard, or vegetable oil
- ½ cup chopped onion
- 2 cups chopped okra, fresh or frozen
- 2 cups peeled chopped canned or fresh plum tomatoes, with juice
- ½ teaspoon salt
- ½ teaspoon freshly ground pepper

1 In a large, heavy skillet, heat the bacon grease over medium heat until a bit of onion sizzles at once. Scatter in the onion and cook, tossing it often, until it is softened, shiny, and fragrant, 3 to 4 minutes.

2 Add the okra, tomatoes, salt, and pepper and stir to combine all the ingredients evenly. Bring them to a gentle boil and then adjust the heat to maintain a gentle simmer. Cook, stirring and scraping to keep the stew from sticking, until the okra is tender and the tomatoes have formed a thick, pleasing red sauce, 20 to 25 minutes. Transfer to a serving dish and serve hot or warm.

Serves 4 to 6

Blue Ridge Mountain Wild Mushroom Bisque

Wild mushrooms thrive throughout the Blue Ridge and Great Smoky Mountains, and chefs and cooks who know their fungi feast on this bounty from spring through fall. North Carolina's agriculture department encourages farmers to cultivate shiitake mushrooms, and Southern grocery stores and farmers' markets nowadays feature mushrooms as an everyday item. Cream of mushroom soup from the iconic red-and-white can was my childhood favorite, and though I still love that soup, I now love making my own version. Mix up the wild mushrooms if you can find them, but don't fret if you can't. Even with everyday buttons, this soup makes a superbly satisfying cold-weather delight.

- ½ cup butter
- 1 cup chopped onion
- 4½ cups coarsely chopped wild, shiitake, or white button mushrooms
- 3 tablespoons all-purpose flour
- 4 cups Chicken Stock (page 152)
- 4 cups milk, evaporated milk, or half-and-half
- 2 teaspoons salt
- ½ teaspoon freshly ground pepper
- ¼ cup Madeira or dry sherry (optional)
- ½ cup finely chopped fresh flat-leaf parsley
- 1 tablespoon chopped fresh thyme, or ½ teaspoon dried thyme

1 In a large saucepan or Dutch oven, melt the butter over medium heat. Add the onion and cook, stirring often, until it softens and becomes translucent, about 2 minutes. Add the mushrooms and continue cooking, stirring often, until they are softened and shiny, 3 to 4 minutes.

2 Add the flour to the onion and mushrooms, and stir to mix it in evenly. Cook, stirring often, for 2 minutes. Add the stock and bring it to a boil. Turn the heat to low and simmer for 10 minutes.

3 Remove the soup from the heat. Transfer it to the work bowl of a food processor. (Or transfer about one-third of the soup to a blender and work in batches.) Pulse and blend it on low speed, for about 1 minute per batch. I like to leave the texture a little bit coarse, but you could also purée it until completely smooth.

4 Return the soup back to the pot, add the milk, salt, and pepper and stir well. Simmer over medium-low heat until the soup is steaming hot, about 10 minutes. Remove the soup from the heat, and stir in the Madeira (if using), parsley, and thyme. Serve the soup hot or warm.

Serves 6

Grandma Harris's Fantastic Turnip, Mustard, and Collard Greens

Thanks to Dr. Jessica B. Harris, the deep, rich culinary history of the African diaspora is ours to know and understand, from geography, agriculture, and religion to migration, ingredients, and reams of traditional recipes. Through her cookbooks, she has brought a world of knowledge to an accessible, enduring place where it can be shared and preserved. Privileged to be her student and fan, and lucky to be her friend, I cook this recipe from her family's table with delight. It's a great greens bonanza from Dr. Harris's grandmother's kitchen, a mighty pot of greens with which to enjoy biscuits or cornbread, salad or steak, salmon or spoon bread. I'm partial to turnip greens, but her grandmother tripled the goodness, mixing together bitey mustard greens, turnip greens, and lots of classic collards. Dr. Harris remembers the enhancements of hot sauce, chopped onions, and vinegar, and the flavor of Grandma Harris's greens: "They were fantastic."

- 4 pounds mixed greens (collards, mustard greens, and turnip greens)
- 8 bacon slices
- 1 teaspoon salt
- 1 teaspoon freshly ground pepper
- Hot sauce for serving
- Chopped onions for serving
- Vinegar, such as balsamic or apple cider, for serving

1 Rinse the greens well in a large bowl or stockpot of cold water. Drain them thoroughly and then trim them, paring away any thick stems and yellowed edges. Tear or cut all the leaves into bite-size pieces and set aside.

2 In a large stockpot, cook the bacon over medium heat until it has rendered its fat and become curly, fragrant, and nicely browned. Remove the bacon and set it aside, leaving the bacon grease coating the bottom of the pot.

3 Pour 6 cups water into the pot and add the greens. Place them over medium-high heat and bring them to a lively boil. Meanwhile, coarsely chop the cooked bacon and add it to the pot.

4 When the water has reached a full boil, lower the heat to maintain a gentle simmer and stir well. Cover the pot and cook, stirring now and then, until the greens are tender and the water has reached a handsome, golden-green hue, about 2 hours. Add the salt and pepper and stir well. Serve the greens and pot likker hot or warm, together, or with greens scooped up into a serving bowl with a slotted spoon, and the pot likker served on the side in its own bowl. Invite guests to season their greens with the hot sauce, onions, and vinegar. ◆

Serves 4 to 6

Maque Choux

This sunny-colored, creamy-crunchy confetti of summertime vegetables comes from the Cajun kitchens of Louisiana. Pronounced "mock-shoo," it's a sauté of yellow corn, pungent onions, sweet bell peppers, and juicy tomatoes, seasoned with green onions and garlic and often made luscious with a kick-off of bacon grease and a rich finish of milk or cream. Its easy-to-find, simple-to-prepare ingredients contrast with its mysterious and incomprehensible name: Maque choux. Translation offers no help: In French, *choux* means "cabbage," an ingredient this dish neither resembles nor contains. Attempts to trace the lineage of *maque* lead nowhere, but the prominence of corn and the resemblance to succotash suggest Native American roots. One thing is clear, this Cajun dish shines as a quick, pretty side dish, or as a main course if you add in shrimp, crawfish, or chunks of ham. While juicy cut-from-the-cob corn is ideal, even corn from the freezer or a can will give you a wonderful, worthy dish.

- 2 tablespoons butter, bacon grease, or vegetable oil
- ¾ cup chopped onion
- ½ cup chopped green bell pepper
- 2 teaspoons chopped garlic
- 4 cups corn kernels, fresh, frozen, or canned (see Note)
- 1 teaspoon salt
- ½ teaspoon freshly ground pepper
- 1½ cups chopped tomatoes
- ½ cup milk
- ¼ cup finely chopped green onions

1 In a large, heavy skillet over medium-high heat, melt the butter, swirling to coat the pan. When the butter is bubbling brightly, scatter in the chopped onion and bell pepper. Cook, tossing and stirring them often, until the onion and bell pepper are shiny, softened, and fragrant, 2 to 3 minutes. Add the garlic and toss well.

2 Add the corn, salt, and pepper. Cook, scooping and tossing to mix everything evenly, 1 minute more. Add the tomatoes and toss to combine them. Lower the heat so that the vegetables are simmering visibly but gently. Cover and cook, stirring occasionally, until the corn is tender and the tomatoes have cooked down to form a rosy-colored sauce, about 15 minutes. Add the milk and cook, tossing often, to mix everything together well. Add the green onions and toss to mix them in evenly. Remove from the heat and serve the maque choux hot or warm.

NOTE: *If you have fresh corn on the cob, remove the husks and silk, and cut each cob crosswise in half. Cut the corn off each cob by running a knife down its sides. To get the creamy white milk, run the back of your knife down the cut surface of the cob, releasing the juice remaining on the cob. Scrape up all the juice from your cutting board, along with the corn, and set it aside for cooking.*

Serves 4 to 6

Sheri Castle's Tomato Gravy

My introduction to the delectable rust-colored biscuit blessing that is tomato gravy came from Sheri Castle, whose writing and teaching about food and cooking keep me smart and well-fed. Born and raised in Boone, North Carolina, Sheri grew up on essential Blue Ridge Mountain dishes like this one, and now that I know about it, I can't imagine how I got by without it. Here, tomatoes and onions are stewed in grease—cooked in a skillet still hot from a batch of bacon, ham, or pork chops that season this simple dish. In summertime, it's a fine variation on our routine lunchtime pleasures of alternating sliced tomatoes with tomato sandwiches. In winter, you can make a wonderful version using premium canned tomatoes. Made with fresh or preserved tomatoes, this easy dish serves up a burst of sunny flavor, enough to turn a biscuit, a pork chop, a plate of rice, or a pile of couscous into a true feast. Bacon grease is traditional, but at Early Girl Eatery in Asheville, they use olive oil and basil with excellent and memorable results.

- 3 cups finely chopped fresh or canned tomatoes, with juice
- Salt
- 2 tablespoons bacon grease, butter, or vegetable oil
- ½ cup finely chopped onion
- 3 tablespoons all-purpose flour
- ½ cup milk
- ½ teaspoon freshly ground pepper

1 In a medium bowl, combine the chopped tomatoes and 1 teaspoon salt and stir well. Set aside.

2 In a large, heavy skillet, heat the bacon grease over medium-high heat, until a bit of onion sizzles at once. Add the onion and cook, tossing it often, until it is shiny, fragrant, and softened, 3 to 4 minutes.

3 Add the flour and cook, stirring constantly, until it thickens into a smooth sauce, about 2 minutes. Adjust the heat if needed to keep it from burning.

4 Add the tomatoes, juice and all, to the skillet and stir them in. Let the gravy come to a gentle but lively boil. Turn the heat to low and simmer, stirring often, for 5 minutes.

5 Add the milk and simmer, stirring constantly, until the gravy thickens nicely. Stir in the pepper and then taste to see if it needs a little more salt. Serve the gravy hot or warm. ❖

9 Basic Recipes *and* Accompaniments

THIS SMALL COMPENDIUM OF RECIPES can provide you with extra goodness as you cook your way through this book. The first two recipes are for stocks. These start your soups and stews off with an extra boost of flavor. Please know I find that commercially available broths work well in my recipes, and using them is a good way to put this book to use in your kitchen.

The remaining seven entries provide recipes for rice, grits, and breads—mostly cornbreads and one special biscuit recipe. Rice comes first, because it is classic with gumbo, the first chapter in the book. I love rice, and eat it often, always making extra since it reheats so well. Grits are one of my favorite foods in the world, as well, and are beloved throughout the South. In many areas, grits are considered to be breakfast food only, while in other places they come with shrimp sautéed in butter or tomato sauce (see page 58) and the long-simmered cutlets known as grillades (see page 96). Here, you'll find an everyday recipe, along with a cheese-infused casserole, which is perfect for company.

There's also cornbread three ways, and my friend Stephanie L. Tyson's fabulous sweet potato biscuits, as an alternative to regular biscuits. This is a starter kit of recipes only, and the list of possible accompaniments for soups and stews is as long as the Mississippi River. Start with couscous, pasta, potato salad, or polenta. Use brown rice instead of white rice, or barley, kasha, or quinoa instead of rice. Saltine crackers work nicely, and toast is not only stylish these days, it's speedy quick.

Whatever you can manage, enjoy every spoonful of your marvelous Southern soups and stews.

Makes 8 to 10 cups

Chicken Stock

Making stock from scratch calls for a modest expenditure of energy and time, but that outlay toward procuring ingredients and tending a kettle goes a long way and yields generous rewards. Cooking the soups and stews in this book will leave you with many of the essential ingredients for great stock, while giving you dozens of reasons—as in recipes—to be grateful you have it on hand. Papery amber onion skins from chopping onions, feathery celery leaves and knobby chunks, carrot tops and peelings, and meaty chicken bones can all team up to flavor your stock. Use chicken legs, wings, backs, and necks, or substitute two meaty carcasses from roasted chickens. Avoid giblets and organ meats, as well as green bell peppers and cruciferous vegetables such as broccoli, cabbage, and kale, because they do not improve in flavor when cooked for a long time. Bay leaves and peppercorns add depth of flavor, as do fresh or dried herbs, which can be added to the stock or simply included in the ultimate destination, a soup or stew you will be making soon. Once you've launched a batch on the stove, you need only check in occasionally, and then pack it up and make storage space for it once it is done and cooled.

- 4 pounds chicken pieces, such as wings, backs, necks, and legs (see Note)
- 3 cups very coarsely chopped onions, including skins
- 2 cups very coarsely chopped carrots, washed but unpeeled
- 1 cup very coarsely chopped celery, with leaves
- 1 teaspoon salt
- 1 gallon water

1 In a large stockpot, combine the chicken pieces, onions, carrots, celery, salt, and water. Bring them to a gentle, lively boil over high heat. Skim off the clouds of foam that float up to and bob on the surface, placing them in a bowl. When the foam has stopped rising, discard the contents of the bowl and lower the heat to maintain a gentle, visible simmer. Fat adds flavor, so leave it in the stock for now.

2 Let the stock simmer, uncovered, for 3 to 4 hours. Remove it from the heat and let it come to room temperature undisturbed. Strain the stock through a wire-mesh strainer into a large container. Cover and refrigerate it for up to 3 days, leaving the fat on top. (It will set up into a golden lid that you can easily move aside when you want to measure out and use some or all of the stock.)

3 To freeze the stock, remove the fat, reserving it for frying and sautéing. Divide the stock among tightly covered containers in useful amounts: quarts, pints, or cups. Or freeze it in ice-cube trays or muffin tins and gather frozen stock cubes into zip-top plastic freezer bags. Seal them airtight and freeze for up to 2 months.

NOTE: *Check with the folks at the meat counter in your favorite supermarket, butcher shop, or at farmers' markets to see if they can supply you with the humbler bony chicken parts, backs, necks, and wings. These impart incredibly fine flavor to stocks and can often be purchased for very reasonable prices.*

Makes about 10 cups

Shrimp Stock

Make shrimp stock at home and you will have a treasure chest of deep, rich flavor for your seafood-based soups and stews. You can make it in advance and keep it frozen in 1-, 2- or 4-cup containers for up to 2 months. You could also make up a batch while you are preparing ingredients for a stew, and then use it in that same dish. Meat stocks benefit from hours of simmering, but shrimp stock blossoms into fantastic flavor in about an hour. The secret is shrimp heads; if you can buy head-on shrimp, do so, and keep heads frozen until you have enough to make stock. For this stock, you can freeze or refrigerate the shrimp for another recipe, since you will need only the heads and shells to make this stock.

- 2½ pounds head-on shrimp
- 1½ cups coarsely chopped onions, including skins
- 2 celery stalks, cut into 2-inch chunks
- 2 medium carrots, peeled and cut into 2-inch chunks
- 1 teaspoon salt
- 3½ quarts water

1 Prepare the shrimp, removing the heads and shells and placing them in a large stockpot. Set the meat aside as you work. Place the meat in an airtight container and refrigerate or freeze it until needed. (You will have about 1¼ pounds peeled raw shrimp to use in a future recipe.)

2 Add the onions, celery, carrots, and salt to the stockpot. Add the water and place the pot over medium-high heat. Bring it to a gentle, lively boil and then lower the heat at once to maintain a gentle simmer. Cook, without stirring, for 45 minutes. If bright red foam rises to the top of the stock, adjust the heat to prevent the stock from boiling over. (You need not skim the foam off.)

3 Remove the pot from the heat and let it cool to room temperature. Strain the stock through a wire-mesh strainer into a large container. Divide the stock among tightly covered containers in useful amounts: quarts, pints, or cups. Or freeze it in ice-cube trays or muffin tins and gather frozen stock cubes into zip-top plastic freezer bags. Seal them airtight and freeze for up to 2 months.

All around the South, people enjoy rice as a frequent side dish and an alternative to mashed potatoes, along with hot biscuits, cornbread, or yeast rolls. In those regions where rice is now or has ever been grown as a cash crop, it remains an essential, common accompaniment to everyday and special-occasion meals. In the Lowcountry of coastal South Carolina and Georgia, rice reigns to this day, especially in the seasoned, broth-based main-course rice dishes known as pilaus or perloos. In the modern rice-growing states of Louisiana, Texas, and Arkansas, salted water cooks it simply and a smidgen of butter often enhances the beloved grain, brought to the table with meaty red beans in New Orleans (see page 126), gumbo (see pages 14 to 31), and etouffée in Cajun country (see page 56). An array of beans, soups, and gravy-kissed dishes are enjoyed throughout these rice-loving states.

Serves 4

Everyday Rice

1 cup long-grain rice

1 teaspoon salt

1 Pour the rice into a medium saucepan with a tight-fitting lid, and add enough water to cover it. Using your hand, swish the rice and water together, and then carefully pour off as much water as you can, without letting any grains of rice escape into the sink.

2 Add the salt and 1½ cups fresh water, and stir them together. Place the pot over medium-high heat and bring it to a lively boil, stirring occasionally.

3 Cook, stirring often, as the rice swells up and changes from a soft ivory color to bright white, and the water level drops down just below the surface of the rice, 3 to 4 minutes.

4 Stir again, and then cover the pot with the lid. Turn the heat to low and cook, covered, for 20 minutes. Remove the pot from the heat and let it stand, covered and undisturbed, for 5 minutes more. Remove the lid and stir gently to release some steam. Serve the rice hot or warm.

Serves 4 to 6

Everyday Grits

Grits have a time-honored place within Southern cuisine. Native Americans thrived on this essential, nourishing corn porridge centuries before colonists set sail from European shores. Made from field corn and cooked to a pleasing, nubby porridge with water and salt, grits grace Southern tables from morning through nightfall, though their strongest place is on the breakfast table accompanied by biscuits, eggs, and something of the salted porcine category. Grits start off as dried field corn, and are traditionally processed one of two ways: The simplest way is to grind whole corn kernels to a very coarse powder between two huge grindstones, making stone-ground grits. The more complex way is to soak the dried field corn in an alkali solution, causing it to soften up, swell, and burst out of its outer hull, forming hominy. Known as *posole* in Mexico, hominy is eaten whole or dried and then ground to make hominy grits. No matter which form they took before milling, raw grits cook up into a wonderful presentation using this recipe. For larger portions, this recipe can be easily doubled.

1 quart water

1 teaspoon salt

1 cup white or yellow grits, preferably stone ground

2 tablespoons butter

1 In a medium saucepan, combine the water and salt and bring them to a rolling boil over medium-high heat. Add the grits in a steady stream, stirring all the while to discourage lumps from forming. Let the water return to a rolling boil, and then stir the grits well.

2 Lower the heat to maintain a gentle, visible boil and cook, stirring often, scraping down the sides and bottom of the pan to encourage an even texture and to avoid burning on the bottom. Cook until the grits have swollen up into a thick, even-textured porridge with a much-softened but still distinctively gritty texture, 25 to 30 minutes. When they are thickened and almost ready, the mixture will blurp and bubble up slowly, reminiscent of lava in a cartoon.

3 Remove the grits from the heat, add the butter, and stir until it melts. Serve the grits hot or warm.

Serves 6 to 8

Grits Casserole with Garlic and Cheese

You could call this a casserole, a soufflé, or a side dish, and each time you'd be right. Close kin to the beloved Southern "vegetable" mainstay, macaroni and cheese, this sunny, satisfyingly substantial dish makes itself welcome and beloved on the buffet table or as a treat to pass at brunch. No reason we need to keep it boxed in to a morning menu, because its goodness and popularity transcend any rules about where people used to slot it. As companion to the array of soups in this book, it has endless possibilities and will win you many new fans. For a handsome dish of corny goodness, you can prepare it close to serving time, as it puffs and falls like a soufflé. It's delicious hot, warm, or at room temp, and while it won't return to its fresh-from-the-oven glory, cut into squares, covered, and reheated gently in a warm oven, it makes a fine accompaniment to a meaty main course or anchors a vegetable plate meal. Hot sauce, whether Texas Pete, Tabasco, or another favorite, is a welcome accompaniment at the table.

- 1 quart water
- 1 cup white or yellow grits, preferably stone ground
- 1½ cups grated Cheddar cheese
- 2 tablespoons butter
- 2 teaspoons finely chopped garlic
- ½ teaspoon salt
- 2 eggs, beaten well
- ⅓ cup milk
- ⅓ cup thinly sliced green onions

1 In a medium saucepan, bring the water to a rolling boil over medium-high heat. Add the grits in a steady stream, stirring all the while to discourage lumps from forming. Let the water return to a rolling boil, and then stir the grits well.

2 Lower the heat to maintain a gentle, visible boil and cook, stirring often, scraping down the sides and bottom of the pan to encourage an even texture and to avoid burning on the bottom. Cook until the grits have swollen up into a thick, even-textured porridge with a much-softened but still distinctively gritty texture, 25 to 30 minutes. When they are thickened and almost ready, the mixture will blurp and bubble up slowly, reminiscent of lava in a cartoon.

3 Remove the grits from the heat. Add the Cheddar cheese, butter, garlic, and salt and stir to mix everything together. Set the grits aside for 10 minutes.

4 Meanwhile, heat the oven to 375°F. Butter a 9-by-13-inch baking pan or a 2-quart casserole dish and set it aside. In a small bowl, combine the eggs, milk, and green onions. Stir with a large spoon or a fork to combine them.

5 Add the egg mixture to the grits and stir to mix everything together evenly. Scrape the grits into the prepared baking pan and bake until they are puffed up and nicely browned, 40 to 50 minutes. Serve the grits hot or warm.

Makes about 15 corn cakes

Corn Cakes

Another reason to keep cornmeal on hand in your kitchen, these handsome little disks of corny goodness work as hand-held flatbreads or fork-friendly soup-and-stew companions. Fry them up in your fat of choice, be it olive oil or canola oil, bacon grease, lard, or butter. Like oven-baked cornbread, these come together at the last minute. Leftover batter keeps well for a day or two, covered and chilled, so make plenty and enjoy another round for breakfast, or as a near-instant accompaniment to a lunch starring last night's Southern stew.

- 2 cups white or yellow cornmeal, preferably stone ground
- 1 teaspoon salt
- 1 teaspoon sugar
- 1 teaspoon baking powder
- 1½ cups milk
- ½ cup water
- 1 egg
- 1 tablespoon butter or shortening, melted, or bacon grease
- 2 to 3 tablespoons vegetable oil

1 In a medium bowl, combine the cornmeal, salt, sugar, and baking powder and use a fork to stir everything together. Add the milk and water and use the fork to blend the liquid and dry ingredients into a batter, just until mixed. A few lumps are fine.

2 Add the egg and mix it into the batter. Add the butter and stir with the fork just until everything is fairly smooth and well combined. Place the batter by the stove.

3 Heat a heavy medium skillet or griddle over medium-high heat until hot. Add about half the vegetable oil and swirl to coat the surface of the pan. When a bit of water sizzles at once when dropped into the pan, spoon in three pancakes, using about 3 tablespoons of batter for each one. Cook them undisturbed until the sides become dry and bubbles form on top, about 1 minute. Carefully turn and cook the other sides until they are nicely browned, about 1 minute more. Transfer the cakes to a serving plate and cover them gently with a kitchen towel. Continue cooking until all the batter is used up, and serve the cakes hot or warm.

Serves 4 to 6

Skillet Cornbread

Nothing beats a pan of hot cornbread coming out of the oven when your bubbling pot of hearty stew is being placed on the table. Whether it's made with white or yellow cornmeal, Southerners have counted on this simple, satisfying staple for centuries, and it's easy to see why. It's made from flint corn or field corn, which thrives in Southern soil and can be easily stored and then ground by hand, by water-driven mill, or by machine when needed. Cornbread requires a bowl, a fork, water, salt, and enough grease or butter to shine the skillet or pan in which you plan to bake it. We love it plain, and we adore it all gussied up with eggs, buttermilk, baking powder, or the crispy fried pork fat bits known as cracklins. You can use cornmeal from the grocery store to make wonderful cornbread, but if you find you really love it, search out some stone-ground old-school cornmeal (see page 169), so you can enjoy this simple, satistfying homemade bread in its most flavorful, classic form.

- 1 tablespoon butter, bacon grease, or lard
- 1 tablespoon vegetable oil
- 2 cups white or yellow cornmeal, preferably stone ground
- 1 teaspoon baking powder
- 1 teaspoon baking soda
- 1 teaspoon sugar
- ½ teaspoon salt
- 2 eggs
- 1½ cups milk

1 Heat the oven to 450°F. In a 9-inch cast-iron skillet (see Note), combine the butter and vegetable oil. Place the skillet in the oven as it heats up, so that the butter can melt and the skillet can become very hot.

2 Meanwhile, in a medium bowl, combine the cornmeal, baking powder, baking soda, sugar, and salt. In another medium bowl, beat the eggs and then stir in the milk. When they are combined, add the milk mixture to the cornmeal and stir just enough to combine them well. Don't overmix; just mix them to a fairly even texture.

3 Carefully remove the hot skillet from the oven and place it on the stove. Swirl to coat the skillet's bottom and sides with the fat. Pour the hot fat into the bowl of batter, leaving enough behind to coat the pan nicely. Set the skillet down, stir the grease quickly into the batter, and then scrape the batter into the hot skillet. Bake for 15 to 20 minutes, until the cornbread is handsomely golden brown, dry, and puffed up.

4 You can serve your cornbread right from the pan, or cut it into serving pieces and transfer it to a serving plate or basket, with a kitchen towel or cloth napkin to keep it warm.

NOTE: *The ideal cornbread pan is a 9-inch cast-iron skillet. If you don't have one now, a lifetime of hot cornbread is reason enough to treat yourself to one, so consider indulging or dropping hints to anyone looking to please you. In fact, any heavyweight skillet with an oven-proof handle works fine, as would an 8- or 9-inch baking pan, square or round. Pouring the batter into a very hot, generously greased cast-iron skillet ensures a handsome, crisp, and delicious golden brown crust on the bottom and a nice rise on the top of the "cake."*

Serves 4 to 6

Spoon Bread

Located right by the intersection of Custard and Soufflé, this beloved Southern accompaniment to a special-occasion feast may find a place among your year-round, borderless repertoire of go-to dishes that expand a meal with minimal effort. Essentially cornbread enhanced with an abundance of eggs, milk, and melted butter, spoon bread comes to the table in a casserole dish or baking pan, to be spooned onto the china plates at Sunday dinner. It can accompany an elegant repast of country ham, fried chicken, or, as Edna Lewis recalls in her eloquent book, *The Taste of Country Cooking*, an early summer menu of sautéed veal kidney with Simpson lettuce and young beet tops. Despite its name, bread would still be called for, either biscuits or yeast rolls. Nineteenth-century spoon bread recipes got their height from eggs alone, often separated so that the stiffly beaten whites provided the lift. Twentieth-century cooks turned to baking powder, which suits me fine. Hot from the oven, spoon bread puffs up beautifully, and then settles down as the minutes pass to a handsome, luscious side dish, delicious hot or warm.

- 1 cup white or yellow cornmeal, preferably stone ground
- 1 teaspoon salt
- 1½ cups boiling water
- 2 teaspoons sugar
- 1 cup milk
- 2 eggs, beaten
- 2 tablespoons butter, melted
- 1 teaspoon baking powder

1 Heat the oven to 350°F. Generously grease a 2-quart baking pan or a round 9-inch cake pan and set aside.

2 In a medium bowl, combine the cornmeal and salt and stir with a fork to mix them together. Pour in the boiling water and stir, scraping the bowl and combining everything into a thick batter.

3 Add the sugar, milk, eggs, and melted butter and stir to mix everything together evenly. Stir in the baking powder, then pour the batter into the prepared pan. Bake for 35 to 45 minutes, until the batter has puffed up nicely and turned a pleasing golden brown. Serve the spoon bread hot or warm.

Makes about 18 biscuits

Stephanie L. Tyson's Sweet Potato Biscuits

These irresistible biscuits come steaming from the oven with the color of sunset and the flavor of candied yams, adding spice notes and tenderness to any meal from breakfast through late-night supper. Their signature ingredient resonates for Chef Stephanie L. Tyson, who named her restaurant after the tuber and includes them on her menu mashed, in risotto, and, naturally, in sweet potato pie. Chef Tyson combines her professional culinary training with kitchen wisdom from a heavenly choir of talented family cooks, and has served superb Southern dishes at Sweet Potatoes restaurant in the Winston-Salem arts district for more than ten years. These biscuits make beautiful music with soups in the vegetables chapter, such as Jenny Fitch's Creamy Spring Greens Soup (page 140), Ruby Lanier's Fresh Corn Soup (page 143), and Blue Ridge Mountain Wild Mushroom Bisque (page 146).

- 2 cups all-purpose flour
- 2 tablespoons sugar
- 1 tablespoon baking powder
- ½ teaspoon salt
- ¼ teaspoon baking soda
- ¼ teaspoon cinnamon
- ¼ teaspoon ground nutmeg
- ¼ teaspoon ground cloves
- ½ cup cold shortening, cubed
- ¼ cup cold butter, cubed, plus 3 tablespoons, melted (optional)
- ¾ cup cooked, mashed sweet potato (see Note)
- ¾ cup buttermilk

1 Heat the oven to 400°F. Grease the bottom of a 9-inch square or round baking pan, or line it with baking parchment. In a medium bowl, combine the flour, sugar, baking powder, salt, baking soda, cinnamon, nutmeg, and cloves. Use a fork to mix everything together evenly.

2 Using a pastry blender, two table knives, or your hands, cut the shortening and cubed butter into the dry ingredients, mashing and pressing until the mixture resembles a coarse meal.

3 In a separate bowl, combine the mashed sweet potato and buttermilk, using a fork to mix them together. Add them to the flour mixture and stir gently just to combine the two. The dough will be very wet.

4 Turn the dough out onto a well-floured work surface. Knead the dough gently, just until it holds together. Pat or roll out the dough ½ to ¾ inch thick. Cut out biscuits using a 2-inch biscuit cutter, and place them gently in the prepared pan. For biscuits with soft sides, place the biscuits close together, almost touching. Otherwise, place them 2 inches apart.

5 Bake until the biscuits are golden brown, 10 to 12 minutes. If you like, brush the biscuits with melted butter. Serve them hot or warm.

NOTE: *For this recipe, you will need about 1 pound of whole sweet potatoes. You can boil them or roast them in a hot oven until tender. Cool, peel, and mash them using a potato masher or a fork, and then cover and chill them for up to 2 days. You could also use canned sweet potatoes, rinsed well and mashed, or prepared sweet potato purée.*

Glossary

Andouille
Cajun sausage, traditionally made from smoked pork shoulder, ground up, seasoned with garlic and chiles, stuffed into casings, and then smoked again. Originating in the French and German communities of Southwest Louisiana, andouille became popular in the 1980s, and is used in such classic Cajun and Creole dishes as gumbo, jambalaya, and red beans and rice.

Bacon
Salty, smoky, and rich with meaty flavor, bacon is made from pork belly that is salted, cured, and smoked. Slab bacon is unsliced and may have skin still attached. Sliced bacon can be standard or thick-cut, and makes an excellent seasoning meat in many soups and stews.

Buttermilk
Traditionally, buttermilk was the tangy liquid remaining once butter had been churned. Southerners have treasured it for centuries, both as a sharp-flavored, refreshing beverage and as an ingredient in baking. It provides flavor and leavening power in baked treasures such as biscuits, cornbread, cakes, and pies. What we purchase today is usually skim milk enhanced with beneficial bacteria to create the desirable astringent flavor and qualities. For an old-school treat my grandfather adored, crumble cold cornbread in a tall glass, pour in buttermilk to cover, and devour with a spoon.

If you don't have buttermilk, add 1 tablespoon apple cider vinegar, white vinegar, lemon juice, or lime juice to 1 cup milk, stir well, and wait 5 minutes. Use as directed in recipes.

Chaurice
This fresh, highly seasoned pork sausage is the Creole Louisiana version of the classic Spanish chorizo (which is a hard-textured air-dried sausage similar to pepperoni and summer sausage). Used in gumbos and other soups and stews from the Creole and Cajun traditions, it has a big following as the ideal sausage for any Creole version of red beans and rice.

Drippings
The soft, thick, semiliquid fat left over from frying bacon, sausage, or other meats. Bacon grease is the classic type of drippings beloved in the Southern kitchen and kept on hand. The drippings from sausage and chicken are often used up at the same meal in the making of gravy, but bacon grease has traditionally been set aside at the back of the stove, often contained in a metal can that once held shortening. Many Southern cooks still keep bacon drippings on hand for seasoning various dishes, but today are more likely to use a covered jar and keep it in the refrigerator.

Fatback
Thick, white fat from the back and sides of a pig. Sometimes known as white meat, fatback comes in two different forms: fresh and salt-cured. Fresh, unsalted fatback can be rendered to produce both lard and cracklins—crispy bits left from frying and used in biscuits and cornbread for flavor and crunch. Salt-cured fatback is a form of salt pork, and is kept on hand as a seasoning meat. It is an inexpensive means of flavoring stews, soups, pots of beans, and greens. Salt-cured fatback is also fried up in cooking oil or lard prior to frying chicken, to enhance its flavor. The same fried fatback then becomes a crispy, crunchy, luscious snack. Salt-cured fatback keeps well in a cool place. Fresh or salt-cured, fatback has no lean meat at all, and is often sold with the skin still attached.

Filé
A seasoning for Cajun and Creole gumbos, filé is made from fresh green leaves of the sassafras tree, which are harvested, dried, and ground to a fine green powder. Originally used in cooking by the Choctaw Nation, filé powder became a prized ingredient in gumbos and other dishes, owing to its thickening characteristics and distinctive flavor. Because it can become stringy when heated directly, filé powder is often added to gumbos and stews just before serving, or at the table, rather than during the cooking time.

Gumbo
A savory stew, cooked in large pots for everyday meals and big celebrations, featuring meat, shellfish, seafood, and an array of vegetables, herbs, and spices. The best-known gumbos are those of Louisiana and the adjoining states along the Gulf Coast. Gulf Coast gumbos are often thickened and flavored with either filé powder, cooked roux, or okra (or a combination of these). Cajun gumbos tend to be hearty, thick, and enhanced with chile heat. Creole gumbos often include tomatoes, and frequently feature okra during the warmer months. The word

gumbo has West African roots, and can mean "okra," or indicate dishes made with okra as a featured ingredient. In the Lowcountry of South Carolina, gumbos traditionally feature shrimp and other seafood, cooked with an abundance of tomatoes and okra.

Hominy
Made from dried field corn, hominy is soaked extensively in potash, a natural form of lye, which causes the corn kernels to swell up into plump, pale, bumpy-looking orbs of a pleasingly firm yet tender texture about the size of a chickpea. Known as *posole* in Mexico, this form of corn is used whole in soups and other dishes. This rotund form of softened corn can also be dried again, and then ground finely to make hominy grits. In Charleston and other areas of South Carolina's Lowcountry, the word *hominy* refers to all cooked grits in their porridge-like form.

Lard
Pork fat, rendered from its solid white state into a semisolid that becomes liquid when heated and serves as a medium for deep-fat frying, sautéing, and adding rich flavor to dishes and cooking methods. Also used in solid creamy form as the fat in biscuits, pie crusts, and sweets. Leaf lard, the fat that surrounds the kidneys, is prized for baking due to its superior quality and delicacy. Commercial lard in supermarkets has many additives and preservatives. Look for lard in specialty food stores, at farmers' markets, and from butcher shops and artisanal meat producers (see page 169).

Salt Pork
This term describes an array of salt-preserved pork products that Southern cooks have long kept handy to season beans, stews, soups, pot likker, and even the oil used for frying chicken. Unlike bacon and ham, it is neither cured nor smoked; only salt preserves it. Included within this category are fatback, side meat, streak o' lean, and small chunks of country ham. Traditionally held at cool pantry temperature, salt pork is best kept wrapped or covered and stored in the refrigerator for several weeks, or in the freezer for several months. You can substitute one type for another in most cases, or use bacon in place of the various forms of salt pork, since it is less salty, assuming you consider bacon's smoky flavor an enhancement, as I do.

She-Crabs
This term denotes female crabs, particularly the blue crab found in abundance in Southern coastal waters, all along the Atlantic coastline, and the Gulf Coast as well. Female blue crabs have reddish-colored tips on their claws, and the aprons on the bellies of male and female crabs differ greatly. Males, or "jimmies," have a vertical, pencil-shaped apron. Younger females, or "sallies," have a triangular apron, while mature females, or "sooks," have an upside-down bowl-shaped apron with a small pointed tip. Mature females may have orange-colored eggs inside their shells, invisible until they are dressed and/or cooked. Taking and eating these crabs is legal, but once female crabs are gravid, with their fertilized eggs protruding from their aprons in a large, sponge-like orange mass, most states prohibit taking them in order to protect the crab population. If they are caught inadvertently, they must be returned to the ocean waters at once.

Side Meat
Salt-preserved pork seasoning meat, side meat is mostly fat but with small portions of lean meat, often thickly sliced and seasoned with pepper. It can resemble bacon, though its fat has a more solid texture. *See* Salt Pork.

Streak o' Lean
Salt-preserved pork seasoning meat, streak o' lean is mostly fat but with significant streaks or portions of lean meat present. *See* Salt Pork.

Tasso
Highly spiced and powerfully smoky, tasso is often called "Cajun ham," although it is made from pork shoulder rather than from the hindquarters of a pig. Salt-cured and then hot-smoked, tasso serves as a robust, intensely flavorful ingredient in Cajun dishes such as jambalaya and gumbo, rather than as a main-course meat. Widely available in southern Louisiana, tasso can be harder to come by outside the region. It keeps well refrigerated or frozen, so consider stocking up for your gumbo pantry (see page 169).

Bibliography

Acheson, Hugh. *A New Turn in the South: Southern Flavors Reinvented for Your Kitchen.* New York: Clarkson Potter, 2011.

Allen, Carol. *Leah Chase: Listen, I Say Like This.* Gretna, LA: Pelican Publishing, 2000.

Anderson, Jean. *A Love Affair with Southern Cooking: Recipes and Recollections.* New York: William Morrow, 2007.

Barker, Ben, and Karen Barker. *Not Afraid of Flavor: Recipes from Magnolia Grill.* Chapel Hill: University of North Carolina Press, 2002.

Bienvenu, Marcelle. *Who's Your Mama, Are You Catholic, and Can You Make a Roux? A Cajun/Creole Family Album Cookbook.* Lafayette, LA: Acadian House Publishing, 2006.

Bienvenu, Marcelle, Carl A. Brasseaux, and Ryan A. Brasseaux. *Stir the Pot: The History of Cajun Cuisine.* New York: Hippocrene Books, 2005.

Brown, Marion. *The Southern Cookbook.* Chapel Hill: University of North Carolina Press, 1951.

Burton, Nathaniel. *Creole Feast: 15 Master Chefs of New Orleans.* New York: Random House, 1978.

Castle, Sheri. *The New Southern Garden Cookbook: Enjoying the Best from Homegrown Gardens, Farmers' Markets, Roadside Stands, and CSA Farm Boxes.* Chapel Hill: University of North Carolina Press, 2011.

Chase, Leah. *And Still I Cook.* Gretna, LA: Pelican Publishing, 2003.

———. *The Dooky Chase Cookbook.* Gretna, LA: Pelican Publishing, 1990.

Council, Mildred. *Mama Dip's Kitchen.* Chapel Hill: University of North Carolina Press, 1999.

Crump, Nancy Carter. *Hearthside Cooking: Early American Southern Cuisine Updated for Today's Hearth and Cookstove.* Chapel Hill: University of North Carolina Press, 2008.

Dabney, Joseph E. *Smokehouse Ham, Spoon Bread, & Scuppernong Wine: The Folklore and Art of Southern Appalachian Cooking.* Nashville: Cumberland House, 1998.

Darden, Norma Jean, and Carole Darden. *Spoonbread and Strawberry Wine: Recipes and Reminiscences of a Family.* New York: Doubleday, 1994.

Davis, Nancy, and Kathy Hart. *Coastal Carolina Cooking.* Chapel Hill: University of North Carolina Press, 1986.

Dragonwagon, Crescent. *The Cornbread Gospels.* New York: Workman, 2007.

Dupree, Nathalie. *New Southern Cooking.* Athens: University of Georgia Press, 2004.

Dupree, Nathalie, and Cynthia Graubart. *Mastering the Art of Southern Cooking.* Salt Lake City: Gibbs Smith, 2012.

Dupree, Nathalie, and Marion Sullivan. *Nathalie Dupree's Shrimp and Grits Cookbook.* Salt Lake City: Gibbs Smith, 2006.

Edge, John T., ed. *A Gracious Plenty: Recipes and Recollections from the American South.* New York: G. P. Putnam's Sons, 1999.

———. *Southern Belly.* Chapel Hill: Algonquin Books, 2007.

Egerton, John. *Side Orders: Small Helpings of Southern Cookery and Culture.* Atlanta: Peachtree Publishers, 1990.

———. *Southern Food: At Home, On the Road, In History.* New York: Alfred A. Knopf, 1987.

Elie, Lolis Eric. *Treme: Stories and Recipes from the Heart of New Orleans.* San Francisco: Chronicle Books, 2013.

Englehardt, Elizabeth. *A Mess of Greens: Southern Gender and Southern Food.* Athens: University of Georgia Press, 2011.

Estes, Rufus. *Rufus Estes' Good Things to Eat: The First Cookbook by an African-American Chef.* Mineola, NY: Dover Publications, Inc., 2004. First published 1911 by the author.

Feibleman, Peter S. *Time-Life Foods of the World: American Cooking, Creole and Acadian.* New York: Time-Life Books, 1971.

Ferguson, Sheila. *Soul Food: Classic Cuisine from the Deep South.* London: Weidenfeld and Nicholson, 1989.

Ferris, Marcie Cohen. *Matzoh Ball Gumbo: Culinary Tales of the Jewish South.* Chapel Hill: University of North Carolina Press, 2005.

Fisher, Abby. *What Mrs. Fisher Knows about Old Southern Cooking.* Bedford, MA: Applewood Books, 1995. First published 1881 by Women's Co-op Printing Office.

Fitch, Jenny. *The Fearrington House Cookbook: A Celebration of Food, Flowers and Herbs.* Chapel Hill: Ventana Press, 1988.

Foose, Martha Hall. *A Southerly Course: Recipes and Stories from Close to Home.* New York: Random House, 2011.

Foster, Sara. *Sara Foster's Southern Kitchen.* New York: Random House, 2011.

Fowler, Damon Lee. *Classical Southern Cooking: A Celebration of the Cuisine of the Old South.* New York: Crown Publishers, 1995.

Grosvenor, Vertamae Smart. *Vibration Cooking or, The Travel Notes of a Geechee Girl.* Athens: University of Georgia Press, 2011. First published 1970 by Doubleday.

Grovener, Yvonne, Cornelia Walker Bailey, and Doc Bill. *The Foods of Georgia's Barrier Islands.* Gainesville, GA: Grovener Bailey Bill, 2004.

Gutierrez, Sandra A. *The New Southern Latino Table: Recipes That Bring Together the Bold and Beloved Flavors of Latin America and the American South.* Chapel Hill: University of North Carolina Press, 2011.

Harris, Jessica B. *High on the Hog: A Culinary Journey from Africa to America.* New York: Bloomsbury USA, 2011.

———. *Iron Pots and Wooden Spoons: Africa's Gifts to New World Cooking.* New York: Fireside, 1989.

———. *The Welcome Table: African-American Heritage Cooking.* New York: Simon & Schuster, 1995.

Height, Dorothy I., and Sue Bailey Thurman. *The Historical Cookbook of the American Negro.* Boston: Beacon Press, 2000. First published 1958 by the National Council of Negro Women.

Hoenig, Pam, ed., and Mark Kelly. *The Lodge Cast Iron Cookbook: A Treasury of Timeless, Delicious Recipes.* Des Moines: Oxmoor House, 2012.

Holmes, Buster. *The Buster Holmes Restaurant Cookbook: New Orleans Handmade Cooking.* Gretna, LA: Pelican Publishing Company, Inc., 1980.

Jenkins, Charlotte. *Gullah Cuisine: By Land and By Sea.* Charleston: Evening Post Publishing, 2010.

Knipple, Paul, and Angela Knipple. *The World in a Skillet: A Food Lover's Tour of the New American South.* Chapel Hill: University of North Carolina Press, 2012.

Lang, Rebecca. *Around the Southern Table: Coming Home to Comforting Meals and Treasured Memories.* New York: Time Home Entertainment, 2012.

Lee, Matt, and Ted Lee. *The Lee Bros. Charleston Kitchen.* New York: Clarkson Potter, 2013.

Lewis, Edna. *The Taste of Country Cooking.* New York: Alfred A. Knopf, 1976.

Lewis, Edna, and Scott Peacock. *The Gift of Southern Cooking: Recipes and Revelations from Two Great American Cooks.* New York: Alfred A. Knopf, 2003.

Link, Donald. *Real Cajun: Rustic Home Cooking from Donald Link's Louisiana.* New York: Random House, 2009.

Meyer, Peter. *Blue Crabs: Catch 'Em, Cook 'Em, Eat 'Em.* Wilmington, NC: Avian-Cetacean Press, 2003.

Miller, Adrian. *Soul Food: The Surprising Story of an American Cuisine, One Plate at a Time.* Chapel Hill: University of North Carolina Press, 2013.

Montgomery, Bertha Vining, and Constance Nabwire. *Cooking the West African Way.* Minneapolis: Lerner Publications, 2001.

Moss, Kay K. *Seeking the Historical Cook: Exploring Eighteenth-Century Southern Foodways.* Columbia: University of South Carolina Press, 2013.

Neal, Bill. *Bill Neal's Southern Cooking.* Chapel Hill: University of North Carolina Press, 1989.

Ogunsanya, Dokpe Lillian. *My Cooking: A West African Cookbook with Tantalizing Family Recipes That Are Deliciously Unique with Robust Flavor.* Austin: Dupsy Enterprises, 1998.

O'Kelley, Sarah, Chris Stewart, and Charles Vincent. *Glass Onion Classics: Recipes from a Southern Restaurant.* Charleston: Soulful Food LLC, 2011.

Opie, Frederick Douglass. *Hog and Hominy: Soul Food from Africa to America.* New York: Columbia University Press, 2008.

Page, Linda Garland, and Eliot Wigginton. *The Foxfire Book of Appalachian Cookery: Regional Memorabilia and Recipes.* New York: E. P. Dutton, Inc., 1984.

The Picayune. The Picayune Creole Cookbook. Mineola, NY: Dover Publications, 1971. First published 1901 by *The Picayune.*

Prudhomme, Paul. *Chef Paul Prudhomme's Louisiana Kitchen.* New York: William Morrow, 1984.

Puckett, Susan. *Eat Drink Delta: A Hungry Traveler's Journey through the Soul of the South.* Athens: University of Georgia Press, 2013.

Puckett, Susan, ed. *The South: The Beautiful Cookbook.* New York: HarperCollins/Weldon Owen, 1996.

Richard, Lena. *The New Orleans Cookbook.* Gretna, LA: Pelican Publishing, 1999. First published 1940 by Houghton Mifflin.

Roahen, Sara. *Gumbo Tales: Finding My Place at the New Orleans Table.* New York: W. W. Norton & Company, 2008.

Roahen, Sara, and John T. Edge. *The Southern Foodways Alliance Community Cookbook.* Athens: University of Georgia Press, 2010.

Robinson, Sallie Ann. *Cookin the Gullah Way, Morning, Morning, Noon, and Night.* Chapel Hill: University of North Carolina Press, 2007.

———. *Gullah Home Cooking the Daufuskie Way: Smokin' Joe Butter Beans, Ol' 'Fuskie Fried Crab Rice, Sticky-Bush Blackberry Dumpling, and Other Sea Island Favorites.* Chapel Hill: University of North Carolina Press, 2003.

Samuelsson, Marcus. *The Soul of a New Cuisine: A Discovery of the Food and Flavors of Africa.* Boston: Houghton Mifflin Harcourt, 2006.

Sanders, Dori. *Dori Sanders' Country Cooking: Recipes and Stories from the Family Farm Stand.* Chapel Hill: Algonquin Books, 1995.

Smith, Bill. *Seasoned in the South: Recipes from Crook's Corner and from Home.* Chapel Hill: Algonquin Books, 2005.

Starr, Kathy. *The Soul of Southern Cooking.* Jackson: University Press of Mississippi, 1989.

Tartan, Beth. *North Carolina and Old Salem Cookery.* Chapel Hill: University of North Carolina Press, 1992.

Taylor, John Martin. *Hoppin' John's Lowcountry Cooking: Recipes and Ruminations from Charleston and the Coastal Plains.* 20th anniversary ed. Chapel Hill: University of North Carolina Press, 2012.

Thiame, Pierre. *Yolele! Recipes from the Heart of Senegal.* New York: Lake Isle Press, 2008.

Tipton-Martin, Toni, ed. *The Blue Grass Cook Book.* Lexington: University Press of Kentucky, 2005.

———. *The Jemima Code: 150 Timeless African American Cookbooks and Their Extraordinary Legacy.* Austin: University of Texas Press, 2015.

Thompson, Fred. *Fred Thompson's Southern Sides Cookbook.* Chapel Hill: University of North Carolina Press, 2012.

Tyson, Stephanie L. *Well, Shut My Mouth! The Sweet Potatoes Restaurant Cookbook.* Winston-Salem: John F. Blair, 2011.

Voltz, Jeanne, and Caroline Stuart. *The Florida Cookbook: From Gulf Coast Gumbo to Key Lime Pie.* New York: Alfred A. Knopf, 1993.

Walter, Eugene. *Time-Life Foods of the World: American Cooking, Southern Style.* New York: Time-Life Books, 1971.

Wiegand, Elizabeth. *The New Blue Ridge Cookbook: Authentic Recipes from Virginia's Highlands to North Carolina's Mountains.* Guilford, CT: Globe Pequot Press, 2010.

———. *The Outer Banks Cookbook: Recipes and Traditions from North Carolina's Barrier Islands.* Guilford, CT: Globe Pequot Press, 2008.

Williams-Forson, Psyche A. *Building Houses out of Chicken Legs: Black Women, Food, and Power.* Chapel Hill: University of North Carolina Press, 2006.

Willis, Virginia. *Bon Appetit, Y'all: Recipes and Stories from Three Generations of Great Southern Cooks.* Berkeley: Ten Speed Press, 2006.

———. *Okra: Savor the South.* Chapel Hill: University of North Carolina Press, 2014.

Woods, Marvin. *The New Low-Country Cooking: 125 Recipes for Coastal Southern Cooking with Innovative Style.* New York: William Morrow, 2000.

Woods, Sylvia, and family. *Sylvia's Soul Food Cookbook: From Hemingway, South Carolina, to Harlem.* New York: William Morrow, 1999.

Mail Order *and* Online Resources

Benton's Smoky Mountain Country Hams
Madisonville, TN
(423) 442-5003
www.bentonshams.com
hams, bacon, and prosciutto

Cajun Grocer
Lafayette, LA
(337) 264-9002
www.cajungrocer.com
andouille, crawfish, and tasso

Camellia Brand Beans
Harahan, LA
(504) 733-8480
www.camelliabrand.com
lima beans, navy beans, red beans, and white beans

Cavendish Game Birds
Springfield, VT
(800) 772-0928
www.vermontquail.com
quail and pheasant

Chef John Folse & Co.
Gonzales, LA
(800) 256-2433
www.jfolse.com
prepared gumbo, jambalaya and boudin, cookbooks, spice mixtures, crawfish, and crab

Comeaux's Inc.
Lafayette, LA
(800) 323-2492
www.comeaux.com
crawfish, gumbo crabs, sausages, and tasso

Hoppin' John's
Charleston, SC
(202) 465-4286
www.hoppinjohns.com
grits, cornmeal, and corn flour

Jacob's World Famous Andouille Sausage
LaPlace, LA
(877) 215-7589
www.cajunsausage.com
andouille sausage, tasso, boudin, dried beans, peppers, spices, and roux

Konriko Company Store
New Iberia, LA
(800) 551-3245
www.conradricemill.com
Louisiana rice and seasonings

Local Harvest
Santa Cruz, CA
(831) 515-5602
www.localharvest.org/store
fresh farmers' market produce network

Lodge Cast Iron
South Pittsburg, TN
(423) 837-7181
www.lodgemfg.com
cast-iron pans, skillets, and griddles

Louisiana Crawfish Co.
Natchitoches, LA
(888) 522-7292
www.lacrawfish.com
andouille, crawfish, shrimp, and tasso

Mariah Jade Shrimp Co.
Chauvin, LA
(800) 445-6119
www.facebook.com/pages/Mariah-Jade-Shrimp-Company-Louisiana-Shrimp/16376464211
crab, crabmeat, oysters, and wild American shrimp

Middleton Made Knives
St. Stephens, SC
(803) 216-1298
www.middletonmadeknives.com
exquisite hand-crafted knives for chefs and home cooks

Penzeys Spices
Wauwatosa, WI
(800) 741-7787
www.penzeys.com
cayenne, dried red pepper flakes, filé powder, thyme, and oregano

Purcell Mountain Farms
Mouie Springs, ID
(208) 267-0627
www.purcellmountainfarms.com
marrow beans, red beans, white beans, and rice

S. Wallace Edwards and Sons
Surry, VA
(800) 222-4267
www.edwardsvaham.com
bacon, ham, salt pork, side meat, and seasoning meats

Wild American Shrimp
(843) 937-0002
www.wildamericanshrimp.com
a network supporting the wild shrimp industry with links to purveyors for wild-caught shrimp from American waters: white, brown, pink, and royal red

Acknowledgments

What a privilege and blessing to work once again with the brilliant, generous publishing team at Chronicle Books. I am grateful beyond measure to my wise, smart, and insightful editor Amy Treadwell; to the creative and tenacious marketing and publicity duo of Peter Perez and David Hawk, and to the rest of the Chronicle Books team: Doug Ogan, Alice Chau, Tera Killip, Steve Kim, and Elizabeth Smith whose work transformed my words and recipes into this handsome, usable, and inviting book. What a gift that, once again, genius photographer Leigh Beisch and company hauled out the pots, pans, ladles, linens, and lenses, stirring up a breathtakingly beautiful feast of images to light up the pages of this book. My heartfelt thanks to Bill LeBlond, former executive editor at Chronicle Books, whose long-ago "yes" to my first book proposal turned me into an author and led to many more projects, including this one. This book and all my work reflect the ongoing company, cheerleading, and support of so many wonderful, precious friends that I can't even list them here, except for one in particular: Jill O'Connor, fellow cookbook author, whose encouragement, smarts, and hilarious outlook keep me thinking, moving forward, and laughing out loud. Nothing would happen for me in this life without my wonderful family. How lucky I am to get to cook for them, and to have them filling our kitchen and home with fun and love.

Index

Table *of* Equivalents

The exact equivalents in the following tables have been rounded for convenience.

Liquid/Dry Measurements

U.S.	METRIC
¼ teaspoon	1.25 milliliters
½ teaspoon	2.5 milliliters
1 teaspoon	5 milliliters
1 tablespoon (3 teaspoons)	15 milliliters
2 tablespoons (1 fluid ounce)	30 milliliters
¼ cup	60 milliliters
⅓ cup	75 milliliters
½ cup	120 milliliters
1 cup	240 milliliters
1 pint (2 cups)	480 milliliters
1 quart (4 cups; 32 ounces)	960 milliliters
1 gallon (4 quarts)	3.8 liters
1 ounce (by weight)	30 grams
1 pound	455 grams
2.5 pounds	1.2 kilograms

Lengths

U.S.	METRIC
⅛ inch	3 millimeters
¼ inch	6 millimeters
½ inch	12 millimeters
1 inch	2.5 centimeters

Oven Temperature

FAHRENHEIT	CELSIUS	GAS
250	120	½
275	140	1
300	150	2
325	165	3
350	180	4
375	190	5
400	200	6
425	220	7
450	230	8
475	240	9
500	260	10